*Dedicated to teachers everywhere
who believe in the quality of education,
and make school days special days*

MY FOLKS AND THE ONE-ROOM SCHOOLHOUSE

*A Treasury of One-Room School Stories
Shared By Capper's Readers*

Capper Press
Topeka, Kansas

Illustration, Design and Production:
Diana J. Edwardson Persell

Editor:
Michele R. Webb

Copyright © 1993
by Capper Press
Second Printing, January 1994
Printed in the United States of America

ISBN: 0-941678-39-3

FOREWORD

"School days, school days, dear old golden rule days, readin' and 'ritin' and 'rithmetic, taught to the tune of a hickory stick ..."
This familiar tune conveys the theme of this latest addition to the dynamic *My Folks* series, the sequel to *My Folks Came In A Covered Wagon* and *My Folks Claimed The Plains*, treasuries of true stories from the pioneer and homesteading eras. *Capper's* call for true tales of readers' experiences growing up with a one-room school education garnered a wonderful response, and the memories captured here are of vital importance to a new generation.

By collecting these warm and often funny stories, we intend to preserve the heritage of the one-room schoolhouses, the strong forerunners of today's educational system. The historical schoolhouse provided much more than the 3 Rs; it served as a focal point for entire communities and provided a generation with a solid foundation upon which to build their lives.

One-room schoolteachers were artists, scientists, musicians, friends, confidantes and janitors. They profoundly influenced the children in their care. It is these educators to whom we dedicate this book.

It is our hope that by reading the letters inside these covers, readers will experience the spirit of the one-room school as it was shared with us. We make no claim of complete historical accuracy; these are purely personal glimpses into the past as it is remembered by those who lived it. In an attempt to maintain the authentic flavor of the letters, few spelling, punctuation or grammatical corrections were made.

We thank and salute our contributors, who made it possible to share this book with a new generation of readers.

Michele Webb
Editor

Memory recalls the old country school,
With many a happy thought,
Where the three R's and strict discipline
Were very effectively taught.

At the crossroads of section sixteen it stood
On a prominent rise of ground.
'twas a sturdy white frame structure
And could be viewed from miles around.

It served as community center
And township meeting hall.
On the north and west the acre was bordered
With willows straight and tall.

The school consisted of grades one through eight,
One room encompassed them all —
Sizes ranged from Brownies and Pigtails
To boys and girls, gangly and tall.

The year was divided in three sessions —
Oft'times a new teacher for every term.
Sometimes the teacher would be very lenient
While another would be consistently firm.

Playground games were numerous
And in progress every day —
We chose up sides right down the line
So everyone got to play.

Baseball, shinny, ante-over,
Just to name a few.
Recess time was much too short
Since we never did get through.

We'd take our sleds in winter
And really got a thrill
Sliding forty miles an hour
Down the side of old sixteen hill.

Or at noon, we'd skate with teacher's consent,
But 'twas really a difficult trick
To get back in time for second bell
When the ice was good on what we called Straw's Crick.

Each year we held a box social
Where young swain would bid on his sweetheart's box,
If he failed, he'd live in mortal fear
That his romance would plummet and land on the rocks.

At the end of each year we'd give a program
And a picnic for parents and friends,
Singing in closing, "How sad the parting,"
As this glorious school year ends.

The one room school had many merits,
Though, no longer by moderns, considered wise.
We learned to study, play, and work together
Regardless of age, sex or size.

I'm proud to make this final statement
Though some may consider me a fool.
I'm glad the foundation for my eduction
Was laid in a one room country school.

        Roscoe E. Armstrong
        Hampton, Iowa

CONTENTS

Chapter 1: *Dear Old Golden Rule*..1

Chapter 2: *School Supplies*..20

Chapter 3: *First Day At School*..27

Chapter 4: *"Reading, 'Riting, And 'Rithmetic"* 38

Chapter 5: *Schoolhouse Cuisine*...46

Chapter 6: *"Taught To The Tune Of A Hickory Stick"*................................54

Chapter 7: *The Wild Kingdom* 72

Chapter 8: *A Tale For All Seasons* 87

Chapter 9: *Special Days* 99

Chapter 10: *From The Teacher* 118

Index 134

CHAPTER 1: "Dear Old Golden Rule"

One-Room Schoolhouse Of Long Ago

Schoolhouses were located near the center of the district served so that none of the children would have more than two and one-half miles or so to walk to get to school. Schoolhouses usually were located on a corner of the "school section" and all were the same general layout. The schoolhouse was a fairly large building with a cloakroom/gear locker just inside the door. This room had hooks for hanging outer clothing, places to store overshoes, lunch pails, brooms, mops, and whatever other equipment and supplies were needed to operate the school.

In the center of the schoolroom there was a large pot-bellied stove; the teacher's desk would be at the back of the room so that all the children's activities could be monitored. The blackboard and the pull-down maps were on the back wall behind the teacher's desk. There was a large unabridged dictionary on a stand, and perhaps a bookcase with a few reference books and story books. In each of these country schools, there was always the potential of needing time and equipment for all eight of the primary grades for which these schools were responsible. Most of the time, however, not more than six of the grades would be represented, with probably two or three students in each grade.

Throughout the school year the schoolhouse became a sort of community center for any public meetings, including Christmas pageants, spelling bees, box socials, pie suppers and any other meetings. Coal oil (kerosene) lamps were provided to light the evening functions. There was a distinctive aroma in all these buildings reminiscent of chalk dust, sweeping compound, lunches of several years and pencil sharpener shavings.

In addition to the schoolhouse, the school grounds consisted of two outdoor pit toilets (one for each sex - sometimes built back to back), a well with a hand pump for drinking water, shelter for the horses ridden or driven hitched to a buggy, sometimes a coal house or woodshed, and perhaps a rudimentary baseball diamond.

Teachers were important members of the community. This highly respected post was frequently filled by young ladies just out of high school. The responsibilities of the job must have seemed overwhelming:

Education of fifteen to twenty students, some of whom could be within four or five years of the age of the teacher, and considerably stronger physically;

Satisfying the parents with the quality of education;

Maintenance of the facility, including pumping water, keeping the fire in the stove in the winter time, doing the janitorial work, and managing the fuel and school supply storage;

Doing the required first aid for the ill and injured;

Mediating the arguments.

During the twenties, the teacher usually boarded with one of the families in the district unless he or she was a member of a local family.

Boys wore bib overalls and ordinary shirts with heavy work shoes to school while girls wore cotton dresses, long black cotton stockings and sensible shoes. During winter weather everyone wore "long johns" underwear. The girls all seemed to have deformed lower legs because the long john legs were impossible to keep smooth inside those long black cotton stockings.

The curriculum was based upon the Three R's (reading, 'riting and 'rithmetic) in the first school years with requirements in Geography, History and Civics (Government) for the upper grades.

Amazing as it seems in 1993, the unsophisticated approach outlined above sufficed as complete education for many people in earlier generations, and provided an adequate base for higher education for many more.

Rex O. Wonnell
San Jose, California

Pay Wasn't Much Then

The old schoolhouses really had just one room, but sometimes one had an entryway where coats and tin drinking cups were hung and lunches were stored until mealtime. Otherwise the coats and cups were hung on nails at the back of the room with lunches placed on a bench near by.

There was a large old wood or coal heating stove in the center of the room. It was the teacher's job to do the janitor work and build and keep the fires. Some of the boys might be persuaded to carry in the wood or coal.

A blackboard was across the front of the room. There were large maps hanging, that could be pulled down like window shades, one at a time for geography lessons.

Bookcases might be on each side at the front of the room, with well-thumbed books. We never had many books so everyone read them all. There was usually a set of World Books. A large dictionary was placed on a small table for everyone's use. A pencil sharpener was probably placed on the wall by one of the windows. There were windows on each side of the room, but children were discouraged from gazing out.

A teacher's desk and chair were at the front of the room with the roll call and grade book on top; also a small school bell which the teacher used to bring the children in from play. A globe was one of the supplies for everyone to share. A dunce stool could be seen setting in the corner, too.

The seats could be either single or double, with a space for books and supplies. In the double seats, two children sat together if the space was needed. The smaller seats near the front were for the younger children and the larger ones at the back were for the older.

School began at 9 a.m. with a 15 minute recess at 10:30. Lunch was from 12 noon to 1 p.m., and another 15 minute recess at 2:30. School dismissed at 4 p.m. The recesses and lunch period allowed plenty of play time for the children. They usually all played together with the teacher participating also.

The drinking water came from a well in the yard with a pump. Each child had his own tin cup. A few really lucky children might have a folding cup.

Two outhouses sat in opposite corners of the back yard, one for the boys and one for the girls. In really olden times, there might be a shed to shelter horses that children or the teacher might ride to school.

The first eight grades were taught by only one teacher. The schoolboard that hired the teacher and took care of any business consisted of three neighbor men. They hired the teacher, bought the wood or coal for fuel, and other items that needed tending to.

The schools were held for eight months. Some that I heard of were for only six months. I guess this was for lack of money to pay the teacher, though the pay wasn't much in those days. In 1920 or earlier, the pay was only about $20.00 per month. In 1938, the pay was about $60.00. In 1945, about $90.00 and in 1950, it was $125.00 per month.

On the last day of school, they usually had a basket dinner for parents and children at the school. Or sometimes, the teacher and pupils went on a picnic to celebrate their freedom from school.

Children in school now could not imagine the schools then, but they learned as much, if not more, then than they do now.
Della Whitesell
El Dorado Springs, Missouri

Teacher Was A Miracle Worker

The teacher of my first one room school was a miracle worker

"DEAR OLD GOLDEN RULE DAYS"

and a wonderful woman.

The schoolhouse was approximately 16 x 24 ft., made of native stone, with the "2 holer" outhouses out by the back fence - the boys as far to the left and the girls as far to the right as possible. Each with its protective panel guarding the doors so no one could see inside when the door was opened.

The school set on approximately one acre of ground with cattle pasture on three sides. On this acre, besides the school and the outhouses, were the school well, a swing set, teeter totter, slide and softball field. Still there was room for marble games, jacks games, little boys digging, and running games and jump ropes.

This school had one teacher and 36 children. The teacher was a miracle worker because the school did not provide a kindergarten. This teacher made a class for the eager five year olds. She had children in all eight grades. Because most 8th grade graduates who went to one room schools could not go to high school, she made classes for the last two years 8th grade students who were interested in more education.

The teacher was also the music teacher, drama teacher, art teacher, speech teacher, lunch room supervisor, custodian, disciplinarian and beloved trusted friend.

Della May Clifford
Garber, Oklahoma

The Daily Routine

In the fall of 1934, while the nation was yet struggling through the big depression, I began my first teaching job at $35 per month.

Being fresh out of high school, with an extra year of teacher's training (which was then a high school subject), the money was good pay and looked good to me at the time.

I still have in my possession the six inch brass bell which was used each morning at 9 a.m., for the 30 minute morning and afternoon recesses, and at the noon hour. At the sound of the bell the children would gather at the steps of the building. The flag would be raised on the flag pole and the allegiance repeated. They they would line up in an orderly fashion and march into the building.

Upon entering the building the children would hang their coats and caps on hooks or nails on the back wall with a shelf above for their lunch pails.

The opening exercises consisted of a Bible reading, recommended by the State Course of Study, followed most times by the Lord's Prayer. To the delight of the children, I would then read 15 or 20 minutes from a book such as *Huckleberry Finn, Tom Sawyer, Rebecca of Sunnybrook Farm*, etc.

By then we were ready to work. All eight grades were represented in the group.

One class at a time would come forward to sit on the long wooden bench in front of the room near the much-used blackboard. While these lessons were given the rest of the pupils would study their assignments for when it came their turn.

At noon someone would work the pump while the rest would take turns washing their hands for lunch.

The teacher usually boarded with a family in the district, maybe for four or five dollars a week. And for sure, she was expected to stay at least one night each school year with each family.

In February of 1937, a tornado completely demolished the little schoolhouse and all of its furnishings and the school year was finished in the basement of the country church nearby. The school was never rebuilt and the pupils were transported to town. It wasn't long afterwards that all country schools were consolidated with town school.

Lena Jump
Marshfield, Missouri

Melting Pot Of Memories

Your request for stories about rural schools stirred many memories. I experienced the Depression in rural Iowa and not only attended three different rural schools, but taught in rural

school five years. Therefore, selecting one incident to write about is most difficult. Should I write about the male teacher who led us in most unusual fun activities during lunch hours; the games we played which I've never seen played elsewhere; the trauma and challenge of entering a new school; program night; or, from my teaching, the morning I entered the building to find that a thief had been there during the night, or that a tramp had slept in the sand table, or of cardinals eating from a sunflower head fastened on a schoolyard fencepost, of nuthatches walking down the trunk of a tree outside the schoolhouse window, a meadowlark surprised from her nest in the tall grass back of the schoolhouse, or. . . . .
Davida Nicholson
Washington, Iowa

Pot-Belly Of The Prairie

In 1906 I was a first grader in our one room country school on the southern Illinois prairie. It was heated by a big pot-bellied stove. Seats for younger pupils surrounded the stove while older pupils occupied those in far corners of the room. They often put on their coats while studying and at the same time we found the heat stifling. A couple of years later we came to school to find old pot-belly gone and seats where it had been. In the corner was a big, round apparatus; they told us it was a jacketed stove. What a difference; far corners of the room were just as warm as the center. I best remember that stove by how glad I was to see it gone.
Florence Palmer
Paris, Illinois

After-School Agenda

After we got home from school the first thing we did was to change our clothes. We put them away for the next day. Every one of us had our chore to do. At night we studied our lessons for the next day. Mama sat by the old wood heater and patched our clothes or darned our socks. Dad read his daily paper and shelled corn for the chickens the next day. Sometimes he helped us with our lessons or played games with us.

Blanche (Silvey) Blevins
Springfield, Missouri

Different Schools — Same Education

One thing I'd like to emphasize is that you received the same kind of education in one of those one-room schools as you did in a graded school. If the school was in New York State, you had to pass Regents in order to enter high school as the children in the graded schools did.

In the school I attended our textbooks were supplied by the district, but in some schools the children had to buy their own.

We had more fun in a one-room school because as soon as noontime was announced we took our lunches and ran outside if it was fair. We went wherever we wanted to go. We very often played in a woods across from the school.

We always had school even if there was a bad storm.

My last fifteen years of teaching were in a graded school. However, I thought I did my best teaching in the one-room school. There, if a child didn't know something such as the six times tables, he was immediately sent into the hall with an older child to learn it. There always was some older child who wasn't busy because the classes lasted such a short time that he was able to get his work done quickly. I didn't send two children into the hall in a graded school because, since they were the same age, they'd probably fool or just visit.

Another example of teaching in a one-room school was that the children did their work in school and not at home. I'd make up questions in social studies. In a graded school most of the children would answer the questions at home. If they couldn't find the answer they'd write "Don't know" or "Can't find." In a one-room school, the child would come to me and say, "I can't find the answer to this question." I'd tell the child where to look, such as, "Look on the top of such and such a page," wherever it was. This helped the child in silent reading as well as in social studies.

Evelina Fuller
Saugerties, New York

Remembering Wood School

At last I was six so I could go to school with my big brother and sister. We walked 1.25 miles to the "Wood School." In nice weather it seemed only a short walk as our friends joined us along the way. But, in winter the snow was often so deep that the big boys had to make a path for us until the crust got hard, then we all walked and slid on top.

Oh, that long underwear, warm bloomers, long stockings, button shoes, button leggings and boots. We took good care of the button hook!

My family taught me to read and do first grade arithmetic at home. So, the teacher gave me about 8 minutes a day to read to her. I loved it. Standing at her desk I read as fast as I could so I could have the next book.

Every spring for May Day the teacher would allow a group of us to go to the meadow where big, long-stemmed purple and white violets grew. We ate our lunch while picking a nice bouquet for the teacher and another to fill our May Baskets for Mother.

We had crayons and water paints and we loved to create beautiful pictures. We were very careful with crayons or colored pencils because there were only a few!

Once in a while the "Big Kids" made candy and popcorn for a 15 minute party.

With eight grades to teach there had to be good discipline. During my 6 years to complete 8 grades the teachers were excellent, friendly and caring. Usually if a pupil wished to cause a disturbance the other children helped the teacher control him.

Classes could last about 10 minutes each, so everyone had to listen and think while the teacher explained a new process or whatever. There were usually only 1 to 5 pupils in a grade so it was easy to help each other and still have time to help the younger ones. In good weather the teacher often allowed 2 or 3 of us to go outside and study together. We studied spelling, orthography, times-tables, or any type of memory work.

Much memorization was required in each grade. We learned many proverbs, Psalm 23, Corinthians 1:13 and other Bible portions and lots of good poetry. When I was in the 8th grade the state required us to study *"The Courtship of Miles Standish"* and *"Hiawatha."* We learned to recite whole sections and even had to be able to write them.

Our library consisted of one bookcase filled with good books and a few reference books. I read everything. I especially remember one series - "The Little Maid of Bunker Hill" and other "Little Maid" books. How I would love to reread them! When I was in the 7th and 8th grades a Mobile Book Bus came once a month to our school. I could have an armful of books for a whole month. What joy!

The State required all 7th and 8th graders in rural schools to pass a test in history, arithmetic, geography and English if we wished to attend high school. This was most unfair! We were herded into a big auditorium in town. Bluebooks (a sort of notebook) and pencils were passed out. The County Superintendent would give instructions, then the test questions were passed. There usually were only 10 questions over a whole book. We were scared, worried and very nervous. Yet very few ever failed and when we went to high school we were never behind the "City Kids" academically.

I'll soon be 79 years old but I'd love to go back to the one room school.

Gladys Cook
Durango, Colorado

As Schools Were Then

Mom belonged to a generation who, if you finished high school and took six weeks of summer school, you were considered good teacher material.

"DEAR OLD GOLDEN RULE DAYS"

She would teach a dozen or so pupils and be paid $40 a month. Not in a bargaining position, she accepted the challenge.

The school board treasurer was a young single farmer in the district. Many of the people in the district were either Polish or Bohemian. Some spoke no English. They were poor - very poor. Routinely the school lunches were dark bread with a slathering of molasses. Not enough clothing and in fact, just not ENOUGH.

Mom noticed that Johnny did everything he could to pester Wally, his kid sister. ONE DAY MOM HAD IT WITH HIM. While now she would be arrested for child abuse, the whack she gave him told him that was enough and more.

The next morning Johnny's mother drove up in a rickety old buggy and motioned Johnny to her. They headed for the school. Mom shook. The woman made a statement in Polish. Johnny translated. "Miss West, my mother says she wants to know if you've had trouble with me." Mom drew a long breath. "Tell your mother I did have, but I'm sure I won't any more."

His mother listened to Mom's words as they came through in Polish. Then she added an explosion of words.

"Mother says that if you can't take care of the trouble, tell her what is wrong and she'll take care of it for you."

"Thank your mother, Johnny, tell her I think we'll get along fine now."

A big smile, a loving pat on Mom's shoulder, and Mom knew she had an ally if she needed one. She didn't. Johnny became her good friend.

Mom was very lonely in this then-isolated area. Then things changed. The Post Office was in the house where Mom boarded. Somehow the young farmer came for his mail more and more during the hours Mom would be there. If nothing else, they had the bond of loneliness. Probably the two best educated people for miles, they became fast friends.

Both went home for Christmas. Mom broke off with the fellow who had been her High School beau. Her friend, during his time at home, broke his engagement. It seems they both had other dreams and they carried them out.

School ended in April. Mom came home with glowing eyes and many plans. June 3, 1914, and the teacher and the school treasurer were married. Mom never taught again, except for her daughter and in Bible School. Mom had only one complaint. "Before we were married that nice young man gave me a check every month, but he stopped!"

       Betty Dernell
       Balsam Lake, Wisconsin

Gypsy Guests

One summer we had a band of gypsies live at the school yard. They would come to our place to buy eggs and milk. They had the full run of the place: two outhouses, a full acre of ground for their horses, playground equipment for their kids to play on, a "storm cellar" in case of tornadoes, a pump and plenty of delicious well water. And all rent free!

       Lola Gilbert
       Mohave Valley, Arizona

Nobody Had Cars

We walked two and three miles to school, most of the schools were where our family farmed. Nobody had cars. We went other places in a buggy or wagon, or all us kids rode horses. We had School break in Summer to do work in the field, and a Fall Break to pick our cotton.

       Dortha Culp
       Sikeston, Missouri

Economy Affected One-Room School

It was 1930 - the year after the crash! Farming communities were struggling with more and harder work to make a living. In their midst the one-room schools were scratching for their very existence. Teachers outnumbered the schools and underbid each other for jobs. Definitely the economy had affected the work and recreation of the one-room school communities. I was fortunate to get a position in a "country" school in this year and I worked hard to keep it.

The young people of the community were starved for evening recreation. For them the school was a place to practice home-talent plays which then brought out the whole community on performance night. The proceeds went to the school.

Since the teacher boarded at a home in the school district, everyone knew where she went, what she did, and whom she dated. But the people of the community also backed the teacher. Their appreciation culminated in the good-time togetherness at the spring picnic on the last day of school.

Verna Gallatin
Marshfield, Wisconsin

Marriage Kept Mum

There was a rule against married teachers those years, so some married and kept it a secret. Young folks I tell this to nowadays can't hardly believe this!

Dorothy Carmann
Riverdale, Nebraska

Hats Off To The One-Room School!

Recently my granddaughter invited me to visit her ultra-modern school. I could not but wonder if students today have any concept of the one-room country schools that served America for more than a century and played a significant role in developing the firm foundation upon which this nation stands - schools that many of their ancestors attended.

The one-room school wore many hats. Its main purpose, of course, was to serve as a place to educate the children of the early settlers, but it was much more than that. The Literary Society, school and community programs, box socials, pie suppers, square dances, and last-day-of-school picnics held there made it the center of community activity.

Above the chalkboard on the front wall a large Seth Thomas

clock faithfully proclaimed the time of day. On the east wall, just above the slate, a Palmer Method alphabet, approximately a foot high, challenged us daily to learn to write both capitals and lower case letters perfectly.

"Background noise" in the one-room school was a geography lesson about the giant pyramids in Egypt, the explanation of a problem in long-division, or how to diagram a simple sentence showing the subject, predicate and object. Slower learners profited from the repetition, quick learners absorbed material far beyond their years.

We learned to be participators. Spelling bees, ciphering matches, states-and-capitals contests, debates - we considered them games. Without realizing we were studying we acquired arithmetic skills, knowledge of geography and a good understanding of the fine contributions made by such men as Thomas Jefferson and John Adams.

We learned early that each individual was important to the team. On the playground, every youngster was included. School sports were not reserved for a few gifted athletes with the rest being merely spectators. Playing fair, taking turns, learning to be good losers as well as winners, all were part of our school day.

Our appetites were whetted for the fine arts. Miss Nielson had a portfolio of large sepia prints of many of the Old Masters... Rembrandt, Monet, Millet, Bonheur, Van Gogh. Each Friday afternoon we gathered around her in a circle, the smaller children sitting cross-legged on the floor, and studied the life of one of the artists and one of his paintings. For three cents, as I remember it, we could purchase a wallet-size print with a brief of the artist's life on the back. That small "art gallery" was a prized possession for years and enriches my life even today.

Miss Nielson trained us in the performing arts. Everyday classroom activity included oral reading. We learned to read clearly, accurately, and expressively. We memorized poetry. We learned to recite before our peers without stage-fright.

The one-room school also gave us social training. Hiring a

"sitter" was unheard of in that day. Children accompanied their parents to all events and were expected to behave. Families set standards for their children and trained them from infancy to meet those standards. The community was an extension of the family.

"You can take the girl out of the country, but you can't take the country out of the girl," goes an old saying. I believe it and thank God for it.

And one of the reasons is the one-room country school.

       Sarah Mitchell Gettys
       Cincinnati, Ohio

The Shrinking Schoolhouse

The one-room school where I attended the first eight years of school still stands, but the queerest thing has happened to it.

When I walked into it, the first grader, fifty-nine years ago, it was the biggest one room building my almost-six-year-old eyes had ever beheld. The rows of double desks were old, and well-scarred with years of carved initials — maybe even my Dad's. The wide boards on the floor were warped so one had to be careful not to drop a precious pencil or crayola lest it roll through the crack. There were some holes that had been drilled near the front of the room to drain mop-water, but they served better as entrance and exit for the field mice.

Two years later a neat hardwood floor had been laid, no holes. Four rows of single desks replaced the old ones. Teacher's old rolltop had been replaced by a flat-topped desk. The old swivel chair, in which I loved to play, had been replaced by a very uninteresting one. There was still plenty of room in the back for a big jacketed stove in one corner, a shelf for lunches and rack for wraps in the other, and room to play games in bad weather.

A few years ago I had the opportunity to show the building to my daughter. "That is the big building you always told me about?" she gasped.

I couldn't believe it either. I expected it to be run down after no school for over thirty years, but the size is what shocked me. You just wouldn't believe how much that old building has shrunk!

Helen Allen
Kansas City, Missouri

(Editor's Note: Mrs. Allen submitted this letter to *Capper's* in 1979, but passed away in July 1992. Permission to use the story was given by Eva Allen.)

The "Menagerie"

Back in those days almost everyone had large families, so several in one family would be going to school at the same time. There were 12 in my family and I have an old report card that says 6 in my family were going at the same time. Four families had the last names of Hawk, Batt, Fish and Miller. Our teacher was Della Miller and she called us her menagerie. On the back of your grade card was a place called "Industrial Work," and listed chores for both boys and girls and your parents gave you a grade on them before signing your card, Also on your card was "Deportment," how you acted in school. The teacher gave you a grade in that, too. The name of the school was Mt. Everett and I was one of the Hawks.

Mrs. Raymond Jobst
Parnell, Missouri

Golden School Days

The Goldenrod is butter yellow; standing there in shame as those who pick its beautiful blossoms are now off to the opening of another school term. I recall when those lovely wild flowers were laden with dust along the road where the Model Ts went merrily along dirt roads. I remember trying to walk within the ruts as I trudged toward the one room rural school. Fall, with its profusion of Goldenrod is a reminder of those days.

Those were lovely days in my early life: my worries were centered on "how could I get the attention of a certain little boy in blue overalls?" Another worry wrinkle might come when I wondered if Ma put enough fried chicken in my syrup bucket so I would have a leg left for the long walk home! Problems inside the books were nothing compared to those stinging problems in the girls out-house....wasp nests and big black ants!

Ah, time has changed the school scene; roads are blacktopped, kids ride a bus to class, hot lunch is served in an air conditioned room and the 3 R's seemed to have taken a back seat to higher kinds of learning. It seems, life is no longer simple...even halls of learning leave me in a daze!

Annabel Whobrey
Rogersville, Missouri

Rural Students Got Individualized Attention

Because there were few pupils in the rural schools, each one got individual attention and help, and thorough drilling in the basics. When they went on to high school in town it was almost sure that the valedictorian and salutatorian of the graduating class would be a former rural school pupil.

Donna Beatty
Arnold, Nebraska

"The Good Old Days"

It was back in the early '30s when I attended a one-room school in the midwest. We were a large family, 6 children in all. We walked to school a couple of miles each way. My folks were paid 30¢ per week per child because we walked to school. Because of this source of income we rarely missed school. In fact, I recall being carried to school in winter because of holes in my shoes. The income from the school kept us in groceries during the depression.

Most of the lessons were learned by "rote"; there were few if any audiovisuals used for teaching but we all six have gotten a good education as we all have good jobs today and none of us have ever received any public assistance. In spite of the hardships, we still refer to those as "the good old days."

Helen Croy
Yuba City, California

MY FOLKS AND THE ONE-ROOM SCHOOLHOUSE

That Old Country Schoolhouse

That old country schoolhouse
Was not like one in city or town,
It's no longer in the spot where it stood
For it has now burned down.

But, oh so many memories linger
About that schoolhouse on the hill,
And even though it is there no more,
In our minds we see it still.

Inside, the pull-down maps were up front,
Pictures of Washington and Lincoln on the wall,
The old bench for lunch buckets to be set,
Our study books were ready for school in the fall.

Most teachers were very nice —
Sometimes a different one each year.
They all did their best to teach us
The importance to learn, they made it clear!

If we failed in getting our lesson,
Perhaps we'd have to stay after school
And we'd soon learn by obedience
That we must respect the teacher's rule.

But there was always time for play.
When noon hour and recess came,
We were all anxious to run outside
And be ready to play some game.

We played baseball, dodgeball,
Blackman, dare base and many more —
What big happy family we were —
Then the bell rang and we headed for the schoolhouse door.

I remember the old heating stove
With a tin jacket all around —
It was there to keep us warm
When the snow was on the ground.

Many a day we walked to school —

"DEAR OLD GOLDEN RULE DAYS"

For there were no school buses then to go —
In the sunshine, rain, and cold,
In all weather, including snow.

School took up at nine o'clock
Five days of each week,
Studying our lessons for the day —
Being dismissed at four, a welcome treat!

Perhaps we'd have a Christmas week vacation
And at Thanksgiving a day or two,
But most of the school term
Was a study course, each day through.

Each Christmas we gave a program
Our parents and neighbors came to enjoy;
Also a pie and box supper was exciting —
Hoping our box would be bought by that favorite boy.

In the yard was the old stile
Just outside the schoolhouse door;
Also trees, the coal shed and water pump —
Why need we ask for more?

We would pledge allegiance to the flag
Outside the door — waving bright and clear
I thank God for that old school
With all these memories I hold dear.

The teachers taught grades one through eight
And for three girls Bernice Fortner, Mildred Shipley, and Edna Flanary
There came a special date
When we had gained the goal to graduate.

Oh what good times with school chums we had!
In my memories they'll always be,
It stood amidst those Amarugia Hills —
That old Oak Grove SchoolHouse District 83.

                                        Edna Flanary Cantrell
                                        Archie, Missouri

CHAPTER 2: School Supplies

Pungent Paste

I was born in 1932, we lived on a farm. Mom had gone to Kansas City to find work, and she moved us into Polo, Mo., from the farm.

We attended a country school near Polo. The school building now sets in town, people now live in it. We walked to school most of the time. I remember the school supplies, nothing smelled like those Crayolas or the paste - Borden's glue of today can't hold a candle to the minty smell of the old paste. Our Big Chief tablets we thought were great, too.

Vera J. Eli
Kansas City, Missouri

Schoolhouse Rock

I just found one of my Momma's boxes with slate pencils inside. What a thrill! I hadn't seen a slate board or slate pencil for years.

In one room schools slate boards and pencils were very important. Tablets and lead pencils were not as plentiful as later. Each student carried his or her own slate board and pencil. If you should lose your pencil you could use a sliver from a slate rock. Slates were used to write individual lessons on. They could be erased and used over. Caution! Both slate boards and pencils break easily. Slate boards came in a variety of sizes and frames. To own one with the frame painted red with Pennsylvania Dutch

SCHOOL SUPPLIES

motif on it has always been my dream.

The "black" boards in the one room school were large framed slate boards. They never wore out, but heavy! Unbelievable! I never could understand why they were thrown out for the more modern chalkboards and chalk. Slate boards were easier to clean with less dust. When washed the slate boards were beautiful!

Della May Clifford
Garber, Oklahoma

Book Boxes Brought Joy

My Mother grew up in South Dakota. She maintained that particular corner of the world was the last to get or do anything and theirs was the last one-room schoolhouse to close. Her parents said it was "only a mile to school," which was probably correct if you cut through cow pastures, crawling under barbed wire fences and keeping a watchful eye out for any ill-tempered bull that might roam the pasture.

Mother liked to tell about the "book boxes." Because there were no libraries available for the students, the county seat would prepare what was called book boxes. They were crate sized, and on the inside cover was a sign up card, much like our library cards. These boxes contained a variety of books to accommodate all students, from grade one through eight. When one school finished with the box, it was rotated to another school. Sometimes when the weather was bad, the box stayed at one school for months. Mother would read every book in the box before it was traded for another.

Eileen Snaza
St. Paul, Minnesota

Kernels Of Knowledge

My memories of a one room country school in southwest Nebraska in 1918:

I had my uncle's slate to use, we had paper tablets - mine was probably 6 by 9 inches. There were bigger ones, probably 9 by 12 inches. Our pencils were penny pencils, cedar wood with a pointed white eraser on the end. Often the teacher would write a word, using chalk on the desk top and we would use kernels of corn to follow the lines.

>Frances Hoyt Trail
>McCook, Nebraska

Alternative "Fuel"

In 1933 we were attending Watson School, a rural school in the Texas Panhandle. Before winter was over, the school ran out of coal. Because of the Depression, there was no money to buy any more coal.

The president of the school board had an old truck with high sideboards. One day he picked up the man teacher and several of the older boys. They went to a nearby ranch and picked up truckloads of cowchips which were unloaded into the school's coal shed. The chips made a hot fire but burned quickly. The teachers had the older boys take turns bringing in a scuttleful of cowchips to keep the school rooms warm. But the word "cowchip" was never mentioned. The teacher would say "fuel."

>Hazel Gohr
>Monte Vista, Colorado

Art For Art's Sake

One corner of a gravel road intersection held a small white-painted building which housed eight grades of Iowa farm children. In summer the grass grew tall around it, the swing chains blew and tangled in the overhead bar and the flag rope banged its metal end against the pole in ringing loneliness.

One last spring session stands out in my memory as we had a particularly progressive teacher that year. For the first time in my life I worked with clay. Its changing properties fascinated me: how it could go from a cold brittle ball to something malleable and responsive to my manipulating fingers.

Rolling the clay into long snakes I soon began to experiment

SCHOOL SUPPLIES

with coils until I had a sort of small mat and then began to build sides around it edges. As it took shape before me I forgot everything else, lost in what was happening before me.

The teacher had been quite supportive of my efforts, especially when she found I had never touched clay before. But at the school display of accomplishments, my mother wanted to know what it was, to which I replied that it wasn't anything but just something I made.

In the typical farm fashion of that time she of course felt that it had to be something or have some purpose, it could not just be. So I searched my mind and called it a round house.

I could see my teacher hovering protectively in the background looking encouragingly on but unable to say anything. So I stuck to my story and called it a round house in spite of the fact that everyone was saying there were no such things.

The teacher and I talked about art and she let me know that things do not always have to have a name and that they can just be for their own sake. Not everything has to have a purpose or use.

Barbara Queen
Rosemead, California

Essential Equipment

If we were to say "sweeping compound" to a modern student, it would be as meaningless to him as "floppy disc" would have been to us, but this mixture of oil and sawdust was necessary for cleaning the old pine floors in early schoolhouses. The one-room teacher, who was also the fire-builder stoker and janitor, would scatter the compound over the floor and then sweep it out along with the dust it gathered up along the way.

The old 2-hole privies with their Sears and Montgomery Ward catalogs were just the same when I went to school as they were when I taught, except that by my teaching years real toilet paper had replaced the catalogs.

Three treasures of my father's school days have survived until now: his slate and two copies of McGuffey's Fifth Reader. My own school days began with a Winston Primer, a lead pencil and a Big Chief writing tablet. I don't think anyone below the fourth grade was allowed to own ink bottles and pens that had to be dipped in ink. Needless to say, blotters were a very necessary part of our equipment.

Marjorie Crouch
Uvalde, Texas

Supplies Depend On Wealth

The early rural schools sometimes had double desks wide enough for two pupils to share. There was always one long recitation bench by the teacher's desk. The blackboard would be on the wall back of her desk with the Palmer method cards of the alphabet in small and capital letters. There would be a box hanging on one wall with big rolls of maps of countries in the world, and a lucky school would also have a globe of the world. There was always two large framed pictures of Washington and Lincoln on the walls to inspire young folks to high goals.

Pupils had to bring pencils, ruler, and a tablet to go to classes in those depression days, and no special school shoes were required for physical education on the playground.

Library books were seldom found in the depression days. The teacher would read a chapter a day for opening exercises from a good book. Books for classes had to be ordered thru the county superintendent's office to assure a sameness in the fourteen subjects offered in the eighth grade.

Supplies often depended on the wealth of the district to obtain them. It was a struggle to juggle classes in all eight grades those early years.

Dorothy Carmann
Riverdale, Nebraska

Inside Our Schoolhouse

With our large "student body," you can imagine all the various sized desks we needed. They needed to be comfortable for a first grader (no kindergarten in those days), all the way to our 5' 5" eighth grade boys. There was the seat, with a desk work space and a shelf underneath for all our "stuff." On top near the top was a groove for our pencils/pens, as the desktops slanted slightly to make easier writing. There was also a hole where we could set a bottle of ink for our fountain pens, or straight pens. One year we had eight first graders and did not have enough small desks for that many. So the fathers built a low table and some benches with backs for that class. We older girls took turns sitting and helping with them. The desks all faced the front (north) of the room where the teacher's desk was located. In front of our desks was a long bench with a back which was the recitation bench. Each class would go there for their "class" time with the teacher.

       Marladeen R. Penner
       Anamosa, Iowa

Coastal Confusion

Our blackboard on the south wall was not slate, but six or eight inch boards fitting tightly together painted black. Our large maps hung above the blackboard. When studying these maps the children knew top was north, and bottom was south, but the east coast of our country was toward the west, and the west coast line toward the east. Soon I learned maps should be on a north wall for less confusion!

       Mrs. Gus Bergstrom
       Griswold, Iowa

(Editor's Note: Mrs. Bergstrom submitted this letter in 1979 to *Capper's*, but passed away in September 1992. Permission to use this letter was given by Lloyd Bergstrom.

For Whom The Bell Tolls

My father was a schoolteacher during the first quarter of this century. He taught in one-room rural schools.

Popa had an old bell, an ordinary one of medium size. It was made of good metal and had a sturdy clapper. Popa rang his bell

MY FOLKS AND THE ONE-ROOM SCHOOLHOUSE

each day of the school term during the twelve years he taught.

In the morning when it was "book time," Popa gave the bell a few quick shakes. Its ting-a-ling officially began the school day. The children already at school put away marbles, homemade bats and string balls, and then ran to the well for a drink. Children not yet at school, but who might be coming down the road, ran hurriedly to the schoolhouse when they heard the familiar ring. No one wanted to be late.

For two hours the children worked busily at their reading and spelling lessons. Then the bell ting-a-linged again. It was time for morning recess.

Recess seemed so short to the children. Just when the score of the town-ball game was getting close, the bell rang. Reluctantly the girls left their playhouses under the trees, their games of "Needle's Eye" and "Sugar Loaf Town." The schoolbell had rung. It was time for arithmetic classes to begin.

Though they really didn't mean it, some of the children said they wished Popa would lose his bell. Playfully, they said it loud enough for him to hear. He turned away and smiled.

Occasionally, some big boy would get bold enough to hide the bell, but there was always some little girl who knew the hiding place. She ran and got the bell and it rang again.

Strange, isn't it, how a simple object like a schoolbell seems, at times, to be a living thing. Popa's bell was this way.

During the twelve years that Popa taught, his bell called to many a child. It welcomed the timid beginner on the first day of school and said good-by to those who finished grade eight at the end of the school year.

Popa's bell hasn't rung for a long time. It sits on a shelf, but it is not forgotten. I'm sure some of the children who were in my father's care can still hear the bell's merry ting-a-ling whenever they recall their happy school days.

O.J. Robertson
Russell Springs, Kentucky

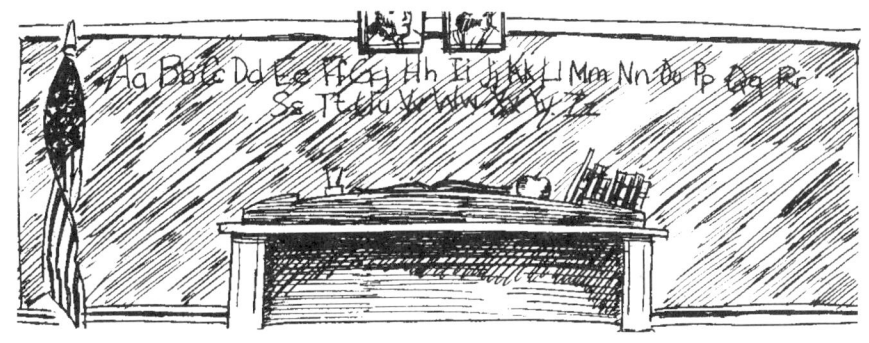

CHAPTER 3: First Day At School

What's In A Name

My mother and father were already the proud parents of five children and looking forward to a new baby. On March 2, 1920, a baby boy arrived. The whole family was trying to decide on a name for him when my mother proudly showed the baby to a long-time friend who said, "Since he was born so close to George Washington's birthday, why not name him George Washington?" George Washington Utterback it was!

Two years later, on February 1, 1922, another boy was born. We all thought, since he was born in February, we should name him Abraham Lincoln.

Our parents were farmers. Because they rented, they, with the children, moved to a different farm every three or four years. In the Spring of 1931 our family moved to a farm several miles away where everyone was strangers. On the first day at the new school, George and Lincoln happened to sit next to one another. The teacher told each child to stand up and give their name. She asked the oldest brother to give his name first, and he said, "George Washington." Then the teacher stepped to the next desk and asked the younger brother his name. When he said, "Abraham Lincoln," all the children laughed. The teacher said, "WE WILL HAVE NO MORE OF THIS FOOLISHNESS!" She grabbed my brother by the shoulder and shook him so hard she tore his shirt. This really hurt his feelings because it was during the depression and they barely had a change of clothing.

My brothers were still upset when they got home from school. They didn't want to go back to THAT school. Nobody had laughed at their names before, plus the teacher's actions had embarrassed them. Our father listened as the brothers recounted what had happened and they he simply said, "Be proud of your names." The brothers finished the term at THAT school, where they made many new friends.

Cecil Utterback Winn
Moberly, Missouri

Starting To School

First days at school were always special as everything had been cleaned, painted, curtains washed, starched and ironed and every family brought their towel and drinking cup. The teacher would write her name on the blackboard and give us a little introduction of herself, and welcome all the pupils and tell what she hoped for us to learn together for the 180-days term of nine months.

Dorothy Carmann
Riverdale, Nebraska

Autumn Anticipation

Anticipating the first day of school in the old one-room country schoolhouse ranked with a day at the county fair or a family reunion. My folks sent off to Sears Roebuck for two new dresses for me to wear on alternate weeks. If a dress got soiled before the week was out, Mother wasn't very happy with me, for laundry was an all-day-once-a-week job forty years ago.

The drugstore at our county seat stocked both new and used books. For farm folks recovering from the Depression, saving 25¢ to 50¢ on a used book was important. If no used book was available for a subject, we children enjoyed fresh pages and fragrant ink for months.

FIRST DAY AT SCHOOL

Being with neighbor children of all ages again was the biggest pleasure. We didn't see each other much during summer, for we lived on scattered farms.

The most awesome aspect of the first day was greeting a new teacher. Our favorite teachers were young, but usually after a year or so they married and moved away. If a teacher were older, we feared she might be cranky, though she seldom was.

At ten o'clock recess most students took a small snack from their lunchpails on the shelf, but I had instructions to save all my food for lunch time. We played ball that first day. Older students chose sides so we younger ones were evenly divided. How we admired the big sixth, seventh and eighth graders.

After ten minutes, the teacher rang the big bell in the tower above the cloakrooms, and we raced back indoors sweaty and refreshed. We all drank from the same dipper, and I recall no serious illness following the unsanitary practice. In later years we were required to have individual cups. Eventually the government provided paper towels, and we lined up for handwashing before we ate lunch. In World War II years, schools were supplied with very tart grapefruit juice and longhorn cheese. The teacher encouraged us to take a little, and I acquired a taste for them.

How delightful the classroom smelled that first day, of new crayons, old yellow paint, slate blackboards on two walls, clean white curtains and oiled floors.

I wish for every child the best of such pleasures as school opens this fall.

       Elaine Carr
       Batavia, Iowa

Tenderfoot Teacher

How well I remember the first school I taught, in 1925.

The first day of school all the children came early to see the new teacher. One child rode a pony, three boys had a horse and cart, the other children had to walk - some quite a distance. At school the chalk boards were not slate. They were wooden boards painted with a black slate coating.

The first day of school I decided to play the school organ and we'd sing "America." When I moved the organ stool the legs fell flat. I found it was set up for a joke and I missed a good fall.

A little first grader became very nervous her first day in school and threw up her lunch all over herself and her desk. I asked myself, "Is this teaching school?"

A mother informed me her son wore a red yarn string around his neck to keep him from having a nose bleed and I was to watch he didn't remove it.

The County Superintendent visited one day. At noon he visited with the pupils. He admired the child's pony and asked, "What do you call your pony?"

The child replied, "Mom said to call it Sleepy because it's slow and lazy like you." The man blushed.

        Inez Warren
        Syracuse, Nebraska

Student "Took A Powder"

Here is my school experience 1915:

Being the youngest of 9 children, I had looked forward to the day I could start to school. That day arrived in 1915 when a man and his wife were the teachers. His wife weighed about two hundred pounds, wore black full skirts down to the floor with white blouses and white embroidered petticoats starched stiff that always showed.

After school started, I held up my hand to go to the outdoor privy to finish my grooming - a little pill box of white talcum powder, using my handkerchief to spread it on my face without a mirror. I felt real confident as I walked into the school room. A boy in third grade across the room stood up pointing his finger at me loudly said "Look at her!" All the students and the teacher looked. The teacher looked like a freight train as she rushed toward me, grabbed my arm, held it high (my feet touched the floor very few times) as she rushed me out to the side room where the bonnets, jackets and shiny dinner buckets were kept.

Up came that black skirt, and those starched, stiff petticoats rubbed my face raw to remove every trace of talcum powder.

That afternoon as school was dismissed the teacher gave each pupil a sample tube of Colgate toothpaste, the first toothpaste we had seen. As we walked home with our treasure, the boys all ate their toothpaste.

How could I ever forget my first day of school?

Mrs. Paul Boyd
Ardmore, Oklahoma

Grungy Greeting

My teaching career began in the Fall before my 18th birthday. My first term was in a country school eleven miles from my home. I had pupils in all eight grades, including eighth graders taller than I, and two dear little Beginners - both girls.

My three-man Board consisted of men who evidently didn't realize how much a new teacher would have appreciated being greeted on her first day by a cleaned school room, so the activities of the first day consisted of scraping two bird nests off the top of the blackboard, emptying desk drawers of field mice homes and babies, dusting and arranging the few precious books, and washing windows and the floor. A note was sent home to the Director that a broken window pane (entrance of the sparrows) needed to be replaced. I took the dingy curtains home to be washed and ironed. Thus ended the first day!

Bessie Lanz
Bassett, Nebraska

Student Got A Hot Seat

My first day at school was a disaster. I got out of my seat, went to the old potbelly stove and stood there whistling while I warmed my backside. The teacher led me back to my seat, and with a paddle really warmed my backside!

Imogene Wyatt
Ashville, Alabama

MY FOLKS AND THE ONE-ROOM SCHOOLHOUSE

Took The Model A Anyway

On my very first day of school, I assumed that on such a momentous big day my mother would give me a ride to school in our Model A Ford. I didn't know my mother as well at 6 as I did in later years. She was a firm disciplinarian, and was not to be swayed from her beliefs. No. I was to walk to school in a grown up manner. So my lunch was packed and I was sent on my way with her very best wishes. Our farm sat back from the road a ways, and it was necessary for me to go down a slight hill, then a long lane, and thence to the main road. As I started down the hill, I spied a dandelion - imagine that, a dandelion in September! That was something I had to show my mother, she would think that was quite unusual also! So I picked the flower and walked back to the house. Somehow she wasn't as impressed as I thought she would be. She gave me a stern lecture that if I didn't start immediately I would be late! So, I started running, and was on my way down the hill when I stubbed my toe and went flying. My dinner pail flew open and out popped my piece of favorite pie, chocolate, as well as the rest of my lunch. It was firmly seasoned with gravel by this time. So, nothing would do but I must go back and get another lunch! I had also skinned my knee in the fall. Well, dear readers, you can imagine the climate in our kitchen by this time. By the time I was repaired, another lunch assembled, and packed, of course my mother HAD to drive me to school......Now in truth, I cannot say that I had deliberately planned this, but that is just the way things worked out.

        Marladeen R. Penner
        Anamosa, Iowa

Reluctant To Miss Threshing Day

The autumn came (1928) when I had to start school, something completely strange and scary. I hadn't played with other children much and felt terribly shy and unhappy about the whole thing. The first couple of days Dad took me with the horse and buggy. But when Dad wanted to leave me at school, that was different.

FIRST DAY AT SCHOOL

He dried my tears with his big red handkerchief and tried to console me.

But the second day was no better; in fact, Dad had a hard time getting me to stay. I thought of all the wonderful happy things going on at the farm and didn't want to be sitting at a school desk. Dad said, "I have to go back, the threshing rig will be coming today, and there's a lot I have to 'tend to before the crew comes to thresh the oats and wheat."

That was just the trouble; I wanted to be there when the threshing machine made its way up our long driveway.

After this long day of school, I ran in my eagerness to get home. I was breathless when I opened the door.

"Can I go out to the granary?"

"Change your clothes first," Mother said. It was still exciting to ride in the grain wagon this year.

The next morning there was the old business of school again; and since the threshers would be starting as early as possible, Dad couldn't take me.

Uncle Bill had arrived to help with the threshing. He said, "Say, Lucy, would you let me drive you to school this morning?"

I looked at him through misty eyes and wondered, I thought Uncle Bill loved me and now he's going to take me to school!

It sure was a good thing that Uncle Bill had a big hanky along, 'cause it was needed to wipe my tears several times before he could get away.

When the second week of school came, I went willingly. Later I went happily. When I was able to read, library books became my favorite stories. The history books contained fascinating information and I could go anywhere in the world via my geography book.

How glad I am that I had the chance to go to school and learn about places all over the world. I'm happy now that I was "forced" to leave the farm when I was six to get some "school-housin'."

Lucille Anton
Circle Pines, Minnesota

Snickers Over Seating

September 1945 found a very eager little 5-year-old girl anxiously starting first grade. Part of the eagerness, just to be with the other kids, especially one "other kid." He was a big, handsome fourth grader and MY BOYFRIEND. Of course, he didn't know that!

We had the type of desks where you could sit with a friend and do your reading, etc. Custom was, girls sit with girls, boys sit with boys. It being my first day of school, I didn't know this. I raised my hand; teacher asked what I wanted; in a loud voice I said, "May I sit with Elwyn?" Needless to say, everyone in the room heard my request and you can imagine the snickers. I don't know who was more embarassed, him or me. Of course, when recess came we took a lot of teasing but it finally wore off.

Earline Mayes
Prague, Oklahoma

New Shoes A Necessity

The first day of school in the country meant new shoes from a catalog since we had gone barefoot all summer. Arriving at the schoolhouse the first day we soon saw that shoes were needed as the yard had grown up in weeds all summer and the mowing machine had left large stubble that could easily cut bare feet.

The schoolroom smelled of varnish as the school board members had varnished the desks and benches making them look almost new.

There was great excitement as we picked the desk we wanted, but usually the teacher soon changed us around. After a week the weed stubble was worn down and we discarded our shoes until cold weather.

The last day of school meant practice for another program and a big dinner. Everyone brought a big box of delicious food. All the mothers tried to outdo each other with their favorite dishes.

Vera Wells
St. Joseph, Missouri

FIRST DAY AT SCHOOL

Paradise Created Problem

First, let me set the stage for a six-year-old's very first day of school. My one-room school was located approximately one mile from our small hired hand's farmhouse. In between our house and the schoolhouse there were umpteen places for a six-year-old to explore. Trees just went on forever, two streams and one small pond. Paradise found.

This setting created a lot of problems for an explorer like me and my dog, Pal, as they started on that very first day of school in 1928.

I was proud as a peacock as I dressed in my brand new Sears Roebuck overalls, a blue shirt, and shoes that needed breaking in. They squeaked when I walked. Mom says, "Now you go straight to school and no dallying along the way."

Well, dallying and I just went hand in hand, especially with my dog, Pal, accompanying me.

We hadn't gone one-quarter mile when a skunk ran across the road ahead of Pal and me. Well now, Pal took after that skunk like a cat after a mouse. The skunk ran into a large culvert that went under the road and Pal was right behind him. I headed for the other end of the culvert and we had him trapped, or so I thought.

I looked into the murky culvert and here they came right at me. Pal was right behind the skunk barking like mad. The skunk was spraying scent every which way as he ran right between my legs and off into the timber with Pal right behind him.

I finally got to school, one-half hour late, and as I entered the warm room, that skunk scent just floated everywhere. Everyone was holding their noses and yelling, "Get out! Get out!"

The teacher sent me to change clothes and I thought to myself, "Boy what's Mom going to say?"

Poor Pal had to be locked in the shed. Mom burned my clothes, and all she said was, "Don't bother the skunks." Moms are like that, you know.

Eugene Carson
Montezuma, Iowa

Made Up For Lost Time

I was nine years old on my first day of school. Polio at one year of age made it impossible for me to walk to school, as all rural kids had to do then. At this time we had rented a farm only 1/4 mile from the school. My sis had taught me to write my name and count. My siblings pulled me to school in a sturdy child's wagon, and as we became acquainted with the kids there I was treated just like the rest. My wagon went up the aisle where I transferred to a seat shared by another. I made two grades the first year and two the second year. At age thirteen I was in the seventh grade up with my peers.

Jewell Cooper
Bolivar, Missouri

Best Seat In The House

As our summer school vacation was coming to a close, it was time to get new dresses, shirts and pants, stockings and shoes, also a new shiny round dinner pail or an empty syrup pail, lead pencils, big chief tablets a new pencil box, a bottle of ink and an ink pen holder and some extra pens.

On the first day there was much excitement. Mother would have dinner pails ready and remind us not to forget anything.

On arrival at school, the teacher would be in the door to greet you. If she or he was new, she would ask your name, age and grade. Then you put your dinner pail on the shelves behind the door. As you go to the desk you had dreamed all summer of occupying, you are in luck - no one had taken the side you wanted, as they were double desks. One liked to sit by the window for a cool breeze.

Mrs. Tone Aalbers
Monroe, Iowa

Ozark Memories

It was hot in late August, and we three sisters walked slowly to keep from kicking up too much dust on our new shoes. Our

FIRST DAY AT SCHOOL

feet weren't used to shoes, anyway, since we'd gone barefoot all summer...except for Sundays, of course.

When we reached the schoolyard we saw many of our friends who lived on neighboring farms. We seldom saw one another in the summer, because most of us helped with the farm work and had little time for playing. Ours was an unusual community, since we had several families who were first generation immigrants. There were German and Swedish friends. These children often spoke with a strong accent, which was looked upon with some curiosity by those of us whose ancestors had settled the area of Verona, Missouri. There were no people of a different color than ours. Some of us had never seen a black or brown or red person, but most of us would have been angry if anyone had considered us backward. We were like the other country kids of that time in that area. There were no consolidated districts. No buses. No cars available to take us to school. We were Ozarks kids, and didn't realize we weren't as well off as anybody!

        Maithel Davenport Martin
        Kansas City, Missouri

CHAPTER 4: "Reading, 'Riting, And 'Rithmetic"

The Three Rs Were The Basics

As with any elementary school, major emphasis was on the Three Rs. It is hard to comprehend how one teacher could lead one class each day for each grade, five days a week, and include all learning experiences suggested for elementary grades. Perhaps we had exceptional teachers.

Basic courses were taught each day. But each of these included much more than its title might suggest. Language included reading, grammar, penmanship, creative writing and an array of other activities.

In all classes, it seems preparation for life was included, and it was expected that often future lives were as farmers.

A class titled agriculture was held once a week for all students fourth grade and up, combined in one class and meeting weekly for the entire year. Content was educational and practical. We were required to measure our own corn cribs, for instance, and determine how many bushels of shucked corn it would hold. Some of the work sounded like conservation or ecology work of today: contour plowing, conserving moisture practices, dry farming, rotation of crops, testing seeds for satisfactory sprouting ability and many other learnings.

It seemed there were countless opportunities to coordinate class activities to reinforce total learning. This was quite an accomplishment to a teacher who was certified to teach directly after high school, providing she had selected "normal" classes in high school. All teachers were single; it was not legal to hire a married woman.

Edna Easter
Independence, Missouri

Students Helped The War Effort

In 1942, when father's family moved to another farm two miles away, they had to attend a different one room school, Logan No. 9. Here the teacher started school each day by reading a chapter out of the Bible and the children all said out loud the Lord's Prayer. Because these were the days of World War II, the school had projects. My father was one of the students who picked the largest amount of milkweed pods and brought them to school, as it was the gathering point. These later were sent away as the inside of the pods was used to make life jackets. My father also helped make slippers for soldiers out of cardboard with flannel sewn around it.

Brenda Fluit
Inwood, Iowa

A Well-Rounded Education

Our curriculum was quite complete. We studied History, Geography, Arithmetic, Reading, Spelling and Penmanship. Scheduling our recitation times for that many classes/subjects must have been a challenge. In smaller schools chances were that there would not be somebody in every grade level. The time for each class was often only 10 minutes or so, and also classes were scheduled so that not all classes met every day. Some met three times a week, and others two times. We were exposed to much information other than our own grade, and so even though we were working on our own assignments, we overheard other information and some of it was bound to soak in by the process of osmosis! The teacher surely did not have time to baby us - she gave us our lesson and from then on we were responsible for it. She did make use of older students in helping the younger ones, which was good for all of us. The older students had two alternatives if they finished their work and had extra time. First—we were all expected to spend a lot of time practicing our penmanship. This was a subject, as the others, and we were tested on it. Secondly, we could spend our time studying for the 8th grade exams.

The other thing I remember, gratefully, is that once a week we had a spelling bee. We were given a good basic phonics course, and then practiced with spelling bees. We were divided into two sides, each with the same number of older and younger students as nearly as possible. Each student was given words suitable to their grade levels. If we missed a word we really should have known we sat down. And so on until only one was left standing that week. You see we were exposed to many words above our level, but they did sink into our subconsciousness, to be called out later. No one was embarrassed because of the tact of the teacher. There was one girl in our school who usually was the winner. Now this was in the 1930s and many farm homes did not have a great deal of reading material for either adults or children. How did she know the words? She studied them constantly from the Montgomery Ward, and Sears and Roebuck catalogs!

Art and music were always taken care of after the last recess on Friday afternoon. For every holiday in nearly every month we gave a program for our parents, and the community in general. This included decorating the schoolroom, making properties for the program, learning short songs, skits and poems pertinent to the coming holiday. I can still sing some of those songs!

Our phys ed activities were surely spontaneous! Many children had to walk quite a ways to school; rural schoolhouses were usually placed so that no student had to walk more than 2 1/2 miles to get there.

Marladeen Penner
Anamosa, Iowa

Neighboring Schools Had Contests

We opened school each morning with "The Lord's Prayer," then I usually read a few chapters from an interesting book, like *Billy Whiskers* or *Dinsmore* or *Tom Swift*.

"READING, 'RITING, AND 'RITHMETIC"

Our favorite thing to do on Friday afternoon was to have a Spelling B or arithmetic contest with one of the neighborhood schools - at that time there was a school situated every two miles.

I do not remember school ever being "called off." When the roads were full of snow the farmers put their horses on the wagon and went through the fields.

Thelma Williamson
Derby, Kansas

Games Taught Skills

We had arithmetic, history, drawing, Palmer method of writing which was great for the author rather than myself, reading, geography, orthography, spelling and home geography, which would be termed science today. We had seeds to plant, and were taught that a funnel cloud was the source of cyclones which dipped down at random to wreak havoc. I understood this from an earlier experience prior to school age. We learned that a tornado was horrible wind blowing in a straight line sparing nothing in its path. Another science experiment was to bring a bottle filled with water. I washed out an empty ink bottle, and with clean water in it, it sure looked handsome. Next morning ice had broken the entire bottom, lifting the bottle up a fraction.

Inclement weather was time for indoor games at recess or noon. IT sat for Poor Pussy while contestants knelt making every cat call imaginable hoping to escape playing IT if IT happened to laugh while petting the contestant's head whilst saying POOR PUSSY.

Royalty was a single time game. The Queen sat wearing a wide brim felt hat. Each subject came in singly to kneel in front of the Queen, and bow their head. When the Queen nodded her head, the victim caught a hatbrim of water to the delight of everyone.

A skill game was made from the end of an orange crate hung diagonal with ten penny nails in a pattern. The center was 25, the numbers from an old calendar were glued under the other nails from 1 to 10, 15, and 20. An exact 100 was a winner, determined by tossing rubber mason jar rings from 7 ft. away. A leader with say 90, if he made over 100 went bust so he had to start all over again hoping to make himself a winner by a quick score from the dozen rings he was allowed each turn.

We had drugs in those days, it was castor oil administered at home, and we did not ask for more.

        Emmett Kirby
        Champaign, Illinois

Graduates Had To Pass The Test

When I started to school (1921-1922) we had the new school house, which cost about $4,000.

In order to graduate from the eighth grade and receive a diploma, we had to take county examinations which were held in our local high schools. In the 7th grade we took tests in these three subjects: Reading, Geography, Physiology. In the 8th grade there were nine subjects: Kansas History, Classics, Agriculture, Writing, Arithmetic, Grammar, US History, Civics and Spelling. We were graded by percentage, with an average of 80% required to graduate. Our graduation ceremony for all in the county who had passed these tests was held in the high school at the county seat. There was an honor roll of those who averaged 90% or above, and as I remember of the top 10 we were asked to be on the program with a reading, music, solo, etc. with no rehearsal beforehand!

        Esther Lewis
        Mission, Kansas

Romance Read Aloud

There were special times, when the teacher played the old pedal organ and we sang. Or when (on Friday afternoons) she would read aloud to us, often from romantic novels of the day. We loved that, because there were very few books in the school other than our study books. TV and movies today are not appreciated half as much as we appreciated those stories.

        Nina Eason
        Denver, Colorado

Early Copiers

The last period on Friday was art - we made things for the windows and bulletin boards and for the fair exhibit. There was no copier - extra copies from a pattern were made with a carbon paper. I grant you they weren't as pretty as the bulletin boards of today, but they were the childrens' work. We stressed penmanship, multiplication tables, etc. No computers or calculators.

Gladys Sybrant
Bassett, Nebraska

Blessed With Fingers And Toes

Five-year-old Donna was being introduced to her first lessons in Mathematics. However, she always used her fingers to count out the sums of her problems.

One day, after calling her attention to the habit repeatedly, I said, "Donna, what would you have done if the good Lord had not given you fingers?"

She smiled and said, "I guess I would have had to count on my toes!"

Madonna Storla
Postville, Iowa

Singing Lesson

When I attended the Little Red Schoolhouse, a memory stands out. I discovered I really loved music in that small room. Mr. Burnett came once a week to teach us the scale and how to use it. The best part of the class was when we all joined in to sing the song he had taught us that day. I loved to sing with my elbows on the desk and my chin in my hands. One day my fingers slid over and pressed my ears closed.

Miraculously I discovered I could hear no one else, only me, singing. I closed my eyes, pressed my ears tightly shut and sang away with the class. Or so I thought. I suddenly felt a tap on the head. My eyes flew open to match my mouth. There was Mr. Burnett standing beside me and all my classmates turned in their seats looking at me and laughing.

"Enjoy your singing better than ours, Jean?" the music teacher asked, laughing, too.

Everyone thought it was so funny. Everyone, that is, but me!

Jean Carpenter Welborn
Tucson, Arizona

County Tests Were Difficult

My first school days were in a small, typical country school near Readlyn, Iowa. We were taught the basics of reading, writing and arithmetic, and both feared and respected the big boys who could scare the smaller pupils. And I learned to keep my mouth shut while sharing a desk with my sister. Whispering was strictly forbidden.

Miss Jolley continued stories from day to day, reading for fifteen minutes after school recess. How we enjoyed them! But when she read the Grimm's Fairy Tales - the forerunner of science fiction, with all the giant-killer stories, I placed my arms on the desk, holding my ears shut. And through this country school teacher we learned to love songs and enjoy singing. During a fifteen minute morning session we learned folk songs, patriotic songs and beautiful hymns. I could belt out all the verses of "The Battle Hymn of the Republic" and such oldies as Stephen Foster's "Massas In The Cold Cold Ground."

In our area, two winters were taken out of our rural education for religious confirmation instruction. It was simply done - no questions asked of school boards. During this time I also studied pamphlets given out by the County Superintendent of schools on all study subjects, questions and answers used in previous county tests. We needed to pass these subjects at the close of our eighth grade to enter high school. I made good grades and also know these tidbits of information stayed with me through many years. I even was published in the local paper, *The Tripoli Leader*.

I believe the country schools were thorough and good in educating in my youth. And I'll always remember a remark made years later at one of my high school class reunions when a

schoolmate remembered those county tests. She was a town kid, and didn't have to take, or pass them - only try them. She reminisced, "I'll have to admit, the country kids were smart - when I took those county tests, I didn't know what I was doing!"
Lucinda Boeckmann
Tripoli, Iowa

Met Literary Giants

It was during the great depression that my father lost all his possessions, his land, the general store, and worst of all, our mother.

My distraught father moved the family to a large house in a rural area, between two towering hills that was two miles to the one-room schoolhouse, leaving small children to trudge their way on rough dirt roads and through creeks of stagnant water and mosquitoes. Perhaps he was unaware of the perils of our journey to and from school.

What a delight to finally arrive at school, and be greeted by a loving teacher, and to have the fellowship of the huddled masses, each from the pits of poverty. There were so few students that we were always ahead in our lessons. On rainy days we were shuffled to the dry side of the building. On wintery days we sat in a circle around the pot-bellied stove. We studied and recited from the greats such as Oliver Goldsmith, Sir Walter Scott, William Wordsworth, Percy Bysshe Shelly and Lord Byron to name a few. This is my basis for the love of literature.

How could I have dared to dream that from that desolate, one-room schoolhouse that I would one day be present in the room once occupied by William Wordsworth at St. John's College at Cambridge, England? Or stand before the original workshop of Lord Byron and Shelly at the foot of the Spanish Stairway at Rome, Italy? The two names immortalized in cement. I shall always remember that I first knew these literary giants in a one-room schoolhouse in the wilderness.
Edna Densford
Albuquerque, New Mexico

CHAPTER 5: Schoolhouse Cuisine

No Complaints Here

For thirty years we had kids in school, and if their complaints about the hot lunches served to them were laid end to end, they would circle the earth! And to think, when I was in grade school, I had never even heard of a hot lunch...

We took our lunches from home, in a bright-colored lunch box if our parents had money, and few did. A lard bucket was next best. Mostly there were paper sacks or newspapers tied with twine. And since paper sacks were not plentiful, we smoothed out our sacks and saved them. We seldom saw wax paper, unless we had a loaf of bought bread and Mother saved the wrapper.

If you happened to have a piece of fried chicken in your lunch, you didn't throw the bone out. Heavens no! You saved it and took it home for your dog or cat. The same went for a crust of bread or a cracker you didn't eat. It seems sort of sad now.

There were no half-pints of milk served with our lunch! If we got thirsty, we went out to the well and pumped a drink of water and everyone used the same cup. (Sometimes a rich kid had a thermos with its own cup, but not often. There weren't many rich kids!)

I considered myself truly blessed if I had crackers and peanut butter. A pickle was a miracle. A piece of candy a rare jewel. How I envied the kids who had lunch meat on bought bread, cookies from the store, and extra things like jars of fruit or candy bars.

When I was in high school and fixed my own lunch, guess what I had!

Elaine Derendinger
Franklin, Missouri

Student Cook

I attended a one-room school in Kansas in the 1940s. True to the times, it had electricity, but no indoor plumbing.

One of the duties of a couple of students at the start of the day was pumping a pail of water from the cistern to fill the school's three-gallon stoneware container. For drinking, a dipper was used to fill the student's own tin cup. Before eating, everyone lined up to take turns soaping hands and holding them over an enamel basin while a student helper poured on cold water for a quick dip 'n rinse.

Then it was time to retrieve the metal lunchbox from the cloakroom cupboard. Lunch brought from home was typically a cold bacon, lunchmeat, or jelly sandwich, a piece of fruit, some potato chips wrapped in wax paper, and homemade cookies. Day in and day out, the same old cold lunch was a monotonous routine.

But country kids could be as modern thinking and innovative as anyone. One year, we students came up with an idea for how to have HOT lunches, somewhat like what the town kids got.

In a storage room there was a portable hot plate. By vote of the 15-member student body, and with teacher approval for a trial period, we instigated the one-room school version of a hot lunch program. I don't recall how good it tasted, but it sure was fun, as one of the older girls, to get to collect and heat up the items from participants, and most of all, to chatter away a few minutes of school time with my friend, the other privileged student "cook."

Carol Darnell
Columbia, Missouri

MY FOLKS AND THE ONE-ROOM SCHOOLHOUSE

"Lunch Stuff" Skills

Attending country school in the one room for my education in school grades one through eight, and having four brothers who also attended classes in the same room for eight years each, I have many memories of fixing school lunches.

Most always we had home-made bread, and slicing it into even pieces was the first chore! The filling to put into each sandwich was of a great variety, but usually home-made butter, with home-made jelly or jam. It was a treat if, once in awhile, we had peanut butter.

Our parents bought no lunch meats, so if we had a meat sandwich it might be cold, whole-hog sausage, or a slice of head cheese (home-made from the meat of a hog's head, feet, and tongue).

I can remember making fried-egg sandwiches, with yolks cooked hard. One of my schoolmates made mustard sandwiches, with just the yellow salad mustard spread over the bread! In the month of May we could have some lettuce sandwiches if our parents got the garden planted early.

There was a really poor family in our neighborhood in the Depression years, and their six children carried their lunch buckets ($1/2$ gallon size tin pails that had contained lard or sorghum). In each might be one small, boiled, unpeeled potato or 2 black walnuts. These children would spend much time peeling their potato or cracking the walnuts out on the front step of the schoolhouse and trying to pick out the nut goodies to munch on. In this way of "slow actions," they could finish "eating" about the same time we all returned our lunch boxes to the hallway shelf. Many times some of us shared bread or a cracker with our friends.

My mother taught me to bake cookies and cake from scratch. Baking in the kitchen range, with the heat from burning cobs or sticks of wood, the cakes would often fall flat. If I managed to produce some treat to put into our school lunch boxes, my brothers never complained.

Sometimes by Thursday or Friday of the week, my ideas and

supplies of "lunch stuff" would be running short. Then I'd think of jello (quick to fix). This would be acceptable only in cold weather, 'cause we had no ice box or refrigerator to cool the liquid jello. Before I could make jello, however, I'd need a cup of boiling water to dissolve the jello powder. My father would say, "You cannot put any more fire in the kitchen stove tonight, there's too much danger of a house fire in the night time." We had no warm water in the house (no faucets, even) so I can remember dipping out a small cup of water and trying to warm it at a living room register. It never did get hot enough to dissolve jello, but I'd stir and stir it and send very rubbery jello for my brothers to eat Friday noon.

I've had lots of experiences packing lunches to eat away from home. During the first ten years of my marriage my husband carried a "lunch bucket" with peanut butter sandwiches, home-made cookies and jello!

Hope Robinson
Yale, Iowa

Stone Soup

I was teaching rural school in the Depression years, and must share with you about the stone soup we made at school one day in winter. One recess we had everyone looking for a large, smooth stone to put into a large pot to make the soup using an old kerosene burner deal I'd brought from home. Two families were to bring some potatoes, one family to bring two large onions, two families to bring carrots and one family volunteered a head of cabbage for next day's soup. Like the story we'd read from the book, a little meat would help the flavor, so I volunteered to bring some "to bring out the flavor of the stone."

During the first recess, a bunch of us got the vegetables ready and put all over the flame to cook until the noon mealtime. It was up to the first graders to wash and scour the stone carefully and place it in the pot. I brought bowls and spoons from home and all said stone soup was indeed a very special treat.

The idea came from the story of the traveler fellow, who went thru the country stopping at places along the way with a smooth white stone always in his pocket. He'd ask the lady of the house to put it in a kettle and make his special stone soup. Then he'd start making suggestions to add vegetables and some meat to bring out the flavor of the stone. All would sit down to a good meal and he'd be refreshed to go on his way again.

But only after he'd fished out the stone to put into his pocket again and thanked the cook for her sharing a meal so he could walk on to spend the night in some farmer's barn.

Dorothy Carmann
Riverdale, Nebraska

Classroom Or Kitchen?

In 1921 I taught in a one-room country school located on the southern Illinois prairie. A big shelf in the back of the room held a large granite kettle, bowls and spoons. Teachers were serving a hot dish to supplement the cold sandwiches in each child's lunch pail. Mothers were happy to furnish ingredients and I had grown up on a nearby farm so cooking for approximately twenty pupils was no problem. Navy bean soup was a favorite and even heat from the top of a jacketed stove provided a splendid spot to cook the beans, I could easily stand on a stool and stir them while listening to a class recite.

Florence Palmer
Marshall, Illinois

Good Ole Days

Depression days in Oklahoma
A time when cash was rare,
A homemade lunch to carry
But we really didn't care.
No store-bought box had we
To hold our meager fare

Of biscuits holding fried eggs

SCHOOLHOUSE CUISINE

Or home-grown slabs of meat,
Perhaps a baked potato -
Either Irish, white, or sweet.
In fall there'd be an apple
Which was a special treat.

A lard bucket or syrup pail
Would hold whate'er we took
To feed ourselves at noontime
Break from poring over our books.
"What's in your lunch today?
Mind if I take a look?"

Warm days we ate outdoors
Clustered with our pals.
Grassy plots or on the stile
Were favorites of the gals.

Some carried milk in a jar,
A thermos was unknown.
Boiled eggs were often cracked
On a friend's noggin bone.
There were some schooldays
When lunch was bread alone.

We enjoyed what food we had
Never knowing we were poor.
Each day the lunch kept us
Until the farmhouse door.
We'd made it through another of
Those "good old days" of yore.

                              Nova Felkins Bailey
                              Beaverton, Oregon

Fried Fish At French Creek

    My mother and I drove to find my new school, it was 16 miles from Waukon. It seemed a long distance, we felt lost and asked a nice man if we were on the right road.

He became my husband June 12, 1929.

The school was in a valley. The birds were singing their beautiful songs and French Creek runs through this valley, it still floods several times a year. The pupils couldn't attend regularly, because of the floods in the creek.

Sometimes at school, we caught suckers (fish) with a butterfly net and fried them on an open fire on racks and ate them with our lunch.

Clara Leppert
Lansing, Iowa

Beans Blew Their Top

Another incident that happened at the country school that was funny: we could take something to warm on the pot bellied heating stove for our lunch. The Messick family had several children in school and used to bring a gallon syrup bucket with beans. One day they didn't get the lid loosened quite enough. Everyone was studying and the lid blew off and plastered the ceiling with beans. No one was burned, which was good as those of us close could easily have been burned with beans. It was close to a program we were having, so the older kids stacked furniture and tried to scrape the beans off the ceiling. The lid really went flying and clanging!

Mildred Jones Waldren
Tribune, Kansas

Bread And Beans On A Snowy Day

The best memory I have is the day every so often when we each brought a little bag of dried beans, brown, white or whatever, and the teacher, Mr. King, brought a large kettle and a piece of bacon and we had a "cook-in" on top of the stove. We older girls took turns keeping an eye on the beans, adding water as needed which was brought from a spring in back of the schoolhouse. We

each brought our own cornbread and whatever else we wanted to eat with our beans. Just imagine the aroma and the taste of cornbread and beans on a cold snowy day! My school, Melton, No. 8.
Gladys Toliver
Orleans, Indiana

Good-Smelling Spuds

Many pleasant memories come to mind, but the most outstanding is the aroma of baked potatoes. We had an exceptionally understanding, kind and thoughtful teacher. Our mothers would send well scrubbed raw potatoes for lunch, and during first recess, which was in the morning, our teacher would climb up on a chair near the large furnace type old stove and arrange the potatoes on top so they could bake while we had our classes. About one-half hour or so later he would climb up again to turn the potatoes and by noon they would be baked just right. What a special treat we thought we had as we broke open the baked potato and let the homemade butter melt over it - ummm, delicious. We had no cafeteria with its many choices as the children have these days, but a delicious treat was made very special because of a caring teacher.
Floranna Krone
Westlake, Ohio

CHAPTER 6:
"Taught To The Tune Of A Hickory Stick"

Fruit Basket Upset

When we were kids in the one room country school 50 years ago, we had a custom called "Fruit Basket Upset" in which we all participated. It happened only once a year, though if a teacher were quite popular, it might happen twice. It was not an event on the school calendar, for only the students knew about it, and it was planned but a day or two in advance. Looking back, I know it startled the teacher and left her with shattered nerves for a while.

Each of us brought a special fruit, an apple, orange, banana or a small sack of nuts. Older students brought extras in case a smaller child forgot. Just after school had taken up, and opening exercises were done, everyone appearing to be settling down to study, the students furtively awaited the signal. The teacher must have wondered at the mischievous glances circulating around the room, though we thought we were being discreet.

An older student was designated to give the signal. When the proper instant arrived - and all of us were nearly bursting with anticipation - he broke the "no talking without permission" rule by saying right out loud and with enthusiasm, "Fruit Basket Upset!"

Each of us reached into desks or pockets for our various fruits, and started them rolling down the aisles of desks toward the teacher's desk. The fruit was rather quiet, and the bananas didn't roll well, but the nuts bounced and rattled on their way with quite a clatter.

The teacher's eyes widened with shock, first at the student speaking without raising his hand for permission, and next at the commotion of rolling fruit.

The event always ended in laughter, and smaller students nearest the front, especially the lively little boys, scrambled on the floor to help the teacher pick up her bounty. She always managed a weak "thank you" for her gifts, and we students eventually settled our minds down for a day of study.

Elaine Carr
Hayden Lake, Idaho

Bloomers Are A Bust

One Saturday our neighbor girl and her classmate went to a girls basketball game in town. The girls' uniforms were big black wide-leg bloomer-type pants and blouses. So on Monday at recess in the afternoon these two eighth grade girls got all girls in a huddle and said, "All that wear black sateen bloomers can play, we will stuff our pleated skirts into our black bloomers and we will have uniforms." So they went behind the board fence and tucked in their skirts and started their game. My sister and I could not play because we had gray flannel bloomers. We felt bad.

But the boys went in and told the teacher to go see what the girls were doing. So she went out and marched them into the schoolhouse and gave them a lecture that modest girls did not show their underwear. So they had to stay after school 20 minutes every night for two weeks. That was once my sister and I were glad we didn't have black bloomers like the rest!

Mrs. Robert Armstrong
Early, Iowa

Smoke Cancelled School

Box Elder, South Dakota, is eight miles east of Rapid City and in 1936 about a dozen families lived there but the school served a wider area of ranches.

I got up early one day with the idea of plugging the chimney so we couldn't have school and to tease the teacher. A dumb idea, but I didn't think about it at age twelve. I climbed to the roof, dragging a bale of hay, and stuffed it in the chimney. When our hard-working teacher lit the stove, smoke filled the room and school was cancelled that day. Later, when she found out who did it, she talked my Dad out of a razor strap treatment. I never forgot her and the gentle lesson of forgiving kindness she taught me.

I was well served by the one-room school system in South Dakota. I am still with the girl I married there 50 years ago.

The Midwest doesn't have the idle dreams of the Sun Belt or the aggressive materialism of the Silicon Valley...it has much more.

William Kunkle
Eugene, Oregon

Discipline At Hickory Grove

I'm writing about my one-room school, Hickory Grove School. My school had desks that seated two pupils, but only one pupil was assigned to each while I attended. The girls were seated on one side of the room and the boys on the other. If a boy was caught throwing spit balls teacher made him sit with a girl of her choice. If caught whispering and it was a girl, she had to sit with a boy. Most embarrassing! It didn't happen often.

Another punishment was to have to stand at the blackboard with your nose in a chalk ring on the blackboard.

Marguerite Schneider
Lenzburg, Illinois

A Family Tradition

It is easy for me to write about the one-room schoolhouse because my siblings and I all spent our grade school years in the same old limestone building attended earlier by both our father and our mother. And I later taught there for 4 years, not too long before it ceased to be a schoolhouse and became a repository for hay.

One of the limestone blocks in this building bore my father's initials, FHN, still clearly visible when I taught there, though they had been carved at least 50 years earlier. My four brothers, one sister, and I, unconcerned about those who would use it, determined to carve our initials on the writing surface of one particular desk: WRN, RFN, FHN, MAN, and MEN. Our youngest brother had a man teacher one year and, after seeing the family lineup, this fellow made up his mind that John's initials would not join the others, but one day they suddenly appeared. JTN had climbed through a window one day when school wasn't in session.

Marjorie Crouch
Uvalde, Texas

Discipline A Necessity

Fifty years ago I taught in a country school named Diamond. With twenty-four pupils and all eight grades, a teacher needed to be in control. One particular day two of my older boys, Luther and Kermit, tried my patience to the limit. I am not even sure now what the incident was, but I judged I needed respect as well as obedience.

The boys were instructed to stoop down, put hands on ankles and lean forward. I proceeded to paddle them and when I was through, I sat down and cried with them.

Several years later Kermit enlisted in the Army and wrote me a letter thanking me for my influence on his life. Later he was killed and I felt sad of his death but glad he served his country and I'd been a part of his life.

The other student is now retired, and at one time we were backyard neighbors. There had been no mention of the paddling until one day I heard him tell his two grandsons, "You'd better be good because that lady was my teacher and she can paddle."

Recently I met "one of my boys" and gave him a big hug. He, too, knew that discipline was and is necessary. Memories like these make teachers proud.

>Euna Vaye Ukena Brant
>Hiawatha, Kansas

Troublemaking Tyrant

I shall begin with my first school experiences in 1912. One mischievous boy liked to play pranks on the girls. One time he put five of us girls on his little pony then made it buck us off. His desk was behind mine. In those days each desk had an inkwell. I had long braided hair that he stuck in his inkwell. I had a pretty new pencil box that I thought a lot of but I broke it over his head. I was sure I'd be in trouble and get punished - but I didn't! I don't remember whether this was the time the teacher tried to whip him or not. He was always doing something not allowed. Everybody was scared he was going to knock the big stove over or he would tear the teacher's dress off.

The big boys had knives that they used to cut switches for the teacher to use for a whip. They were kept in the corner back of the book shelves to remind us of our behavior.

>Emma May Schell Carroll
>Jasper, Missouri

Schoolhouse In Red

The schoolhouse was a red one, which is the only right color for a country school. This color is a blend of authority and excitement and keeps a boy's mind on where he is supposed to go. It saves him from getting lost in apple orchards, hay stacks and such other small heavens as might coax a boy to forget about school. It takes a strong color to put a young head in books and keep it there, when poems are growing up all about him. And so these schools are best painted the color of discipline.

First you should know that in those days our water supply was kept in a grey earthen jug. There was a faucet that spilled into the wash basin beneath. On this afternoon, for one reason or another, the wash dish was filled with a mixture of soapy mud and a little water - the usual residue from several pairs of hands at recess time. No one had bothered to empty it.

One of the older boys had just raised the sign that, in 1944 would have stood for Victory to Mr. Churchill, but in 1920 meant only "May I leave the room?" Permission was not granted because Teacher sensed that this boy's objective was not so much personal as merely a chance to get out of answering the multiplication tables. Now it was necessary back in those days to have some system by which the teacher could control the comings and goings of children who had to leave the room. Near the door were two cards - one for boys and one for girls. Whenever one left the room he or she turned the appropriate card to read "Out"; when the pupil returned the card was reversed to read "In." This controlled the rural system, indicating whether one could leave the room or not. Only when the sign showed "In" could you receive permission to go "Out."

Well, since this smarty was foiled in his attempt to get out of arithmetic, his nose and ears became pointed like a fox's, and on his way to the blackboard he slyly turned the girls' card to read "Out" - thus forestalling any girl from asking to leave. For the rest of the morning the hair-ribboned side of the room had to stay put, for none of them dared to raise her hand to tell the teacher that the sign was wrong.

But at noon recess one finally did tell the teacher and named the culprit who had juggled the card. Teacher told him to march right up to her desk. She reached for her heavy hickory ruler. He started up the aisle, taking forever to get there. This naturally exasperated our good lady beyond all patience and at that precise moment when teacher, boy and wash basin came into a straight line, she grabbed up a geography book from the corner of her desk and flung it at his head. That book flapped its wings like a blue heron and took off dead on the target. But instinct, like a kingfisher, can outfly the heron and it reached him first. He ducked. Asia, Africa, North America, South America, Europe and

Australia continued on overhead and straight on down into the muddy waters of the basin. We could not keep our laughter behind our teeth. No one could except the teacher. She was chagrined, and desperately trying to salvage some victory for herself, she told him that it served him right, seeing as how it was his own geography text. A little uncertain, he stooped down and separated the continents from the puddle on the floor. Then he made a discovery. He gave the book a swipe on the seat of his pants as Smarty came all smart again, marched in triumph to her desk and held it out to her. It was the teacher's book!

     Ralph W. Seager
     Penn Yan, New York
Reprinted with permission from THE SOUND OF AN ECHO.

Third Time's The Charm

My husband likes to tell this story about his days in a one-room country school.

In his school there were 33 boys and girls ranging in age from five to 16, as many of the farm boys went to school in the winter to keep from having to help their fathers put up the wood for fuel. Also they liked picking on the pretty young teachers who were unable to cope with so many big boys as well as the little beginners.

Having successfully "run off" two young ladies in one year, the director hired Mr. Anson, thinking a man would be able to keep order. This was quite a challenge, but soon the boys were able to win his confidence and got him to play games outside with them.

One day they were playing "hide and seek" and one boy coaxed him into the woodshed. With him safely inside, he locked the door from the outside, keeping him there until 4 o'clock when they let him out and all went home.

The teacher quite naturally was angry and frustrated as he was not quite sure whether he should report the incident. Strange as it may be, the very next day the same thing happened as the boys promised not to do such a thing again. Even the third day the same thing was in progress when an angry parent came on the scene and caught them in the act. It seems there was a little girl who had "tattled," thus ending their "vacation."

At the end of the term another teacher came who was able to take care of any situation. Naturally there were not so many big boys attending that year.

Mrs. Glen Oliver
Moorhead, Iowa

Let Sleeping Teacher Lie

Prairie Dell, the one-room school I attended from September, 1921, to April, 1929, was located on the northeast section of Piatt County, Illinois.

One year a young man was our teacher. The children were playing outside during the last recess. A hot south wind was blowing that September afternoon. I was thirsty and went inside to get my drinking cup. I crept back outside and told the children the teacher was asleep on the recitation bench. One of the boys said, "He went to see his girl last night. Let's play a trick on him."

The older boys untied the two ponies from the fence beside the stile, and tied them to the fence back of the boys' toilet. All were very quiet. The teacher soon came outside to the front step and rang the bell long and hard. The children didn't make a sound. The teacher locked the schoolhouse door, got into his Model-T Ford, and left. Some of us, including me, felt guilty. We could not get inside to get our dinner pails. So we went home.

Mrs. Guyneth Walker
Atwood, Illinois

A Spanking for Nell

If you were to attend a one room schoolhouse, like so many of the country children did, you would find it quite different from the schools you attend today.

In that one room the teacher had to be very strict, in order to be able to teach so many different grades. When she told you not to do something, you didn't do it. If you did you were punished. Some of the methods were: keeping you after school, missing your playtime, or last but not least a spanking. If you got one in school, you most likely got one when you arrived home.

One day at noon, while everyone was outside playing, some of the older boys had a ladder and placed it up the side of a shed. This was where the wood was kept for the stove. The teacher had warned us the next one to climb up would be spanked. Since I had played with my brothers I wasn't afraid of most things. The boys dared me to climb the ladder. You guessed it, I did. Did the teacher spank me? Yes she did!

Mildred Swinford
Keokuk, Iowa

Double The Trouble

All children had chores to do after school, like feeding the animals or cleaning the horse stables, splitting wood for the cook stove for Mother to bake and get our meals, get oil in for the kerosene lamp and study our homework.

One rule was if you get a spanking in school you'd get two of them when you got home!

Henry J. Meyer
Hudson, Michigan

How To Make A Spitball

Thinking of school brings me back to around 1914 when I started to school. We were excited about our new clothes, our shoes, long stockings, gingham and calico dresses and sateen bloomers. Everything was made by our mother that could be. That was quite a chore for a mother with four daughters.

At school there was mischief among the boys. They liked to make paper wads and flip them to the ceiling or each other when the teacher was not looking. To make a good paper wad you chew a piece of paper until you get it just right, and this is when it is real juicy. You then put it on the end of your finger and flip it with your thumb. If it is a good one it will land on the ceiling and splatter out. Sometimes there were quite a few in sight. I can still see them. They would tear out pages of poems so they would not have to memorize them. When the girls went to the toilet they threw rocks at the toilet. They did not always get by with these things - I can still remember being outside and hearing that old whip stripping their legs.

Blanche (Silvey) Blevins
Springfield, Missouri

Arithmetic For Punishment

When I first started school, teacher had a "hickory stick" to punish urchins. Later teachers used "Stay in at recess," or "Stay after school" as punishment.

Everybody had horses, there were no automobiles in those days. In summer they had buggies and wagons. In winter, they had cutters and bobsleds which we called "bobs." Roads were not paved and there were no snowplows

One of our pastimes in winter was what we called "Hooking Bobs." We would grab a ride on a "bob" going one direction and ride it until we met one coming the other direction and ride back. The farmers did not mind us riding their sleds like that. One day there was no bob coming the other way. We were late getting back. That year we had a teacher who used the Arithmetic Book for punishment. She told us, "Take your seats and take out your Arithmetic books." She started with the youngest and assigned problems until we all had assignments. She finished with, "And hand them in before you go home today." That was the only time I had Arithmetic for punishment.

Mary Gardener
Forest Park, Illinois

Hot Cross Buns

My brother, sister and I were attending a one room rural school in Jefferson County, Iowa. My brother was one of the "big boys," I was in the third grade and my sister was in her first year of school. It was a very cold day in winter. The coal burning heater in the center of the room was burning fiercely. Pupils near it were much too warm while those sitting near windows or outer walls were chilly, a condition common to uninsulated schoolrooms heated in this fashion.

My brother was a mischief-maker and somewhat of a leader among the older boys. He seldom was caught in the act, however. On this particular day his best friend, Rusty, was caught in some misdeed. She told him to stand beside the red hot stove and kept him standing there until wafts of smoke actually began to rise from his bib overalls. When that was called to Miss Joseph's attention, his punishment ended. (I think as I write - what a lawsuit would arise from such punishment today!) It certainly was cruel treatment, but I do not remember Miss Joseph as an unkind teacher. I believe she was not fully aware of the intensity of the heat (her desk was not near the stove) and that she was rather desperate in her need to control the older boys.

Davida B. Nicholson
Washington, Iowa

Timid Trespassers

My cousins and I vowed we would never, ever trespass again.

My father's people had driven all the way through the County to our farm for a reunion. What a meal! Our aunts must have tried to out-do each other with their casseroles and baking.

In the afternoon, we cousins usually played hide and seek or something, but we were too stuffed. We checked out the tire swing, and the new animals and nests, when someone noticed the one-room schoolhouse high upon the bluff across the meadow.

"Let's go see it," said John.

"Oh no. Dad says not to trespass."

"Well, let's walk off this big dinner, anyway." Of course, he steered us to the road that led up the long hill, and around the huge curve to the schoolhouse. It was so hot and dusty. We flopped in the shade. Soon we younger ones saw gophers to chase. Buffalo Beans and flowers were picked. The boys checked out play equipment and outbuildings.

"Have you ever been inside?" Onno asked

"Oh, yes," I bragged. "When Dad mows the schoolyard, he unlocks the door so Clare and I can get out of the sun. We play school while we wait for Dad."

"Let's go in and play school!"

"Oh no. It's locked and it wouldn't be right!"

But they were already checking windows. Soon everyone was pushed or pulled over the sill. The room sounded hollow. And smelled musty. It was scary. We knew we shouldn't be there.

Chugga! Chugga! Chugga! A car was coming! But why? No one ever drove up here. Maybe somebody called the Sheriff. We made a dash for the window, all trying to climb out at once.

Chugga, chugga! It was closer. And louder and louder. Would it stop? It came over the crest and around the curve, and went on by and down the next hill! We ran home, and, as I said before, we vowed never, ever to trespass again.

Dorothy Klahn
Denver, Colorado

Teacher Got Last Laugh

This happened in my last year of teaching. It was Halloween time and every year the kids would drag up an old outhouse to put on the steps right against the door so I couldn't unlock it. Also they would go around behind and tie up the rope so I couldn't ring the 8:30 bell. So I had to call the school board to help me get in each time.

So some of my friends decided we would wait until they had done all the damage, so we pulled the outhouse off just so I could unlock my door. Then we went around and crawled up the ladder (which they left standing), and untied the rope so when I came the next morning I went in and rang the 8:30 bell.

Here come all the kids (with their mouths hanging open) and they come in the room and said, "Miss McDonald, how did you get in here?" And I said, "I just unlocked the door and came in."

"How did you ring the 8:30 bell?"

"Just like I always do."

A little later I was putting some work on the blackboard (my back was turned) and I heard someone say, "...and we can't find the ladder anywhere." My gang had hidden the ladder in an alley and they found it later. Anyway, we got the last laugh.

     Emilie Bird
     Beatrice, Nebraska

Tricked For A Treat

I first attended school in a little one room schoolhouse in 1901. I had many experiences there during my school years. One I especially remember involved my best friend's uncle, a very strict man, who was teaching at the school. It was just before Christmas and it was the custom of all of the teachers to "treat" each of the kids with a bag of candy just before school let out for the holidays. Our teacher, however, had hinted that he was not going to "treat." When the older boys learned of this, they decided they would get their candy one way or another. So when the teacher went to the nearby coal shed, the boys skipped over and locked the coal shed door behind him. He pounded on the door and demanded to get out, but they refused to let him out until he promised to "treat." As it turned out, and to the boys' embarrassment, our teacher had planned all along to give us candy.

     Edith Willcut
     Mound City, Kansas

(Editor's Note: Mrs. Willcut wrote this letter to *Heart of the Home* in 1979, but has passed away. This story is reprinted with permission by E.R. Willcut.)

Held Back For Hanky Panky

The first school I ever went to was a country school. I was a first grader, only girl in my class. There was one little boy in school and he was in my class, we got along fine at recess. With a rope around my waist he held the other ends in his hands and drove me around the schoolyard. Next time it was his turn and he was my horse, but as soon as the teacher rang the bell to start classes we went to our seats - but not to study. We would make faces at each other and laugh out loud, so she moved us one on one side of the stove and one on the other. But we would peek around, make a face and laugh out loud. Then she made us come to the blackboard, she drew a circle and told me to put my nose in it. Freddy was told to do the same. We were good until she turned her back, then we were up to the same old tricks. Needless to say, I never passed that year.

       Mrs. Moody Messick
       Marysville, Kansas

The Whispering Campaign

My second year of teaching I accepted a position in a school of 26 students. Five girls and 21 boys, hence my older sister warned me I was asking for trouble. Talk about waving the red flag in front of the bull! I was determined to succeed and thought I was, when a whispering campaign started during recesses and noon hours. When I approached a group of students they laughed and broke up, only to regroup at a more distant area.

Twinkling eyes and sly grins led me to believe trouble was afoot and the longer it went on the more nervous I became. Finally one morning as I called my students to order, the biggest boy in school stood up and started approaching my desk. Others followed suit, each carrying a piece of fruit or a candy bar and singing Happy Birthday!

       Fern Kenkel
       Woodbine, Iowa

For Their Ears Only

Miss Banks had been the teacher in our little one room country school for so many years people had forgotten when she first started teaching there. I had been going to her for six years that I had been in school. This was a beautiful fall day and I was glad to be back in school, so in a playful mood I started to act up. Miss Banks had moved over to the door and I didn't stop to see that she went out the door. I jumped up and said in a loud whisper, "Where's Granny?" Something made me look over my shoulder and my face broke out in perspiration. Miss Banks was standing there. She laid a cool hand on my brow and said, softly, "Is it too warm in here for you dear?"

Helen Vance
Cortez, Colorado

A Punishment For Every Crime

When I was in the third grade my pencil wrote a note to someone else with naughty words and the teacher had me stay after school that Friday afternoon. She gave me a sound spanking with the paddle. I think it was the only time I got punished at school.

Another type of punishment was to write something one hundred times or be assigned a week's job of dusting erasers or carrying out trash to a barrel burner.

Dorothy Carmann
Riverdale, Nebraska

She Coveted Crayons

We lived on a farm on top of a steep hill about 1/4 mile from the school. All the little kids, or so I thought, had a box of crayons. Crayolas, we called them then. Lord, how I wanted a box of Crayolas. The only way I knew how to get them was to steal them. I'm sure I had never stole anything before and trust me, I haven't since. The teacher was boarding with us at the time, she must have told Mom about it. Anyway, Mama, as we called her, said, "Berniece, go get your Crayolas and come with me." She went to the back yard and broke off a big limb from a peach tree, stripped off all of the leaves and said, "Come with me." She made me walk down that big ol' hill in front of her. She wrapped that peach tree limb around my poor skinny legs every step of the way there back to the schoolhouse. Once there, I put the box of Crayolas through a crack in the door. Back up the hill Mama and I went, and she didn't miss a lick.

Berniece Wilson
Poplar Bluff, Missouri

No Bluff On Him

There was a family that attended our one-room school, that gave the lady teacher so much trouble that the school board hired a big rough man teacher.

That family did not get their bluff in on him. At the end of the first school year the teacher told us he hadn't been nearly as hard on us as he was going to be the next year.

I worried about that all summer. I begged my mother to let me stay home the next year. I promised to do the washing, baby sitting and about all the work if I didn't have to go to school. She said I had to go to school. It turned out the teacher wasn't any harder on us than the year before.

Jeneal Riley
Rogers, Arkansas

Closet Scamps

I am sure that there were times that the teacher had to muster up courage to unlock the deserted school building and enter it, for it was a well-known fact that sometimes tramps slept in the schoolhouse if they gained entrance, or in the coalhouse.

We played a prank one morning which did nothing to bolster our teacher's confidence. We arrived before the teacher drove up in her Model A. One window had a piece of glass broken out, so one of us was lifted up to reach in and unlock the window. The four of us crawled in through the opened window and hid in the dark corner closet. We didn't have to wait long before we heard a key in the door. Our teacher went immediately to the closet to hang her coat, and as she opened the door we all yelled, "Boo!"

The poor lady raised a foot off the floor. We should have been punished severely but our dear teacher just laughed with us at our big joke. She resigned at the end of the year. I like to think it wasn't because of us.

> Jeanette Larson
> Story City, Iowa

No Gum Allowed

Pupils were corrected by the teacher in those days. One main punishment was standing on the floor at the front of the room, or remaining in their seats at recess or noon. One instance I remember was when the teacher made a rule that no chewing gum was allowed in school. This person forgot, and as punishment had to stand on the floor with upraised arm pointing at a picture in the room for an hour.

> Frances Gump
> Clarksburg, Missouri

Little Doc And The Heater

Little Doc wasn't really old enough to go to school, but they let him go just to get him out of the way. Homer was real quiet and interested in learning but Doc was real hyper and just a-fidgeting all the time. He'd slip up next to the other fella on the bench next to him and push him off the end of the bench. He was doing something like this all the time. So Ella (the teacher) made him sit on the floor and count his toes and fingers.

There was a big heater in the back of the church (which served as a school). When you took the lid off of it, it was like looking down in a barrel. Ella said, "Doc, I can't do anything with you — I'm just gonna put you in the heater." (It was in July.) She took him by the hand and led him back to the heater. He had great big black eyes and he began to shine them eyes. Ella took the top off the heater, picked up Doc and set him down inside it. He screamed for just about a minute. She raised the lid up and looked down at him and said, "Now are you going to be a better boy?" He promised he would, so she took him out of the

heater. Doc joked about this from time to time later in his adult life.
Gerald D. Massey
Blanchard, Louisiana

Hilarious Hold-Up

My dad whittled out a wooden gun for my brother John, who loved it so much he took it to school to show it off. John was quite a cut-up, so when school took up he raised his hand. When the teacher asked what he wanted, he asked her if she had heard of the big "hold up." When she said no, he told her, "My gun's holding the window up!" John was sitting by a window, and he had propped the window up with his wooden gun. His schoolmates had a big laugh, but the teacher didn't think it was so funny. She kept him after school!
Velma C. Young
Maywood, Nebraska

CHAPTER 7: The Wild Kingdom

This Little Piggy Went To School

I had to walk over a mile to school. In bad weather I would ride my pony. Our school did not have a barn. When I arrived at school I would tie up the reins to the saddle horn, tell her to go home, and smack her on the rump. She would run home where my folks would put her into the barn. About a half hour before school was out my folks would saddle her, tie up the reins, tell her to go to school, and smack her on the rump. She would run to school, arriving before school was out. First she would stop at the door and whinny. Then she would walk to the window where she could see me and wait until I started to the door. She always beat me back to the door. She loved to run so we always raced the wind home.

The animal the children seem to love most at our one room country school was a white sow piglet named Betty Coleen. Betty was an orphan who had been raised from birth by a 10-year-old girl. This piglet followed the girl everywhere. When she could escape the family yard she would quietly follow the girl to school. Betty liked to lie and let the children scratch her ears and stomach. Until the teacher discovered her! The teacher would send the little girl home, Betty following close behind her. Sometimes her mother would let the girl stay home. (She would have walked over 3 miles that morning.) Sometimes the mother would saddle a horse and take her back to school. It would then be a while before

Betty would get to visit school again. When Betty became a mother most of the little girls at school wanted a baby pig.

Della May Clifford
Garber, Oklahoma

Bump In The Night

One evening after school I borrowed my brother-in law's Model T Ford to go into town about 5^1/$_2$ miles to get some drawing paper and supplies. (For anything beyond the bare necessities the teacher had to furnish it out of her meager salary.) This was open range. Quite large herds of cattle roamed the prairies. It got dark before I started home and as you may know the Model T didn't have a good lighting system. The light didn't shine very far ahead. While I was driving I felt a bump and then another bump. The car was working all right, I finally could see that there was a herd of cattle that decided to bed down for the night in the middle of the road. I made it home okay and we had the art lesson the next day.

Kathrine Schwynock
Salem, Oregon

Schoolyard Visitors

One day we had a real experience in anxiety - a bull in the schoolyard. Everyone was afraid to go to the outhouse and we just wanted him to move on. The teacher went out and waved at him shouting "shoo!" He was annoyed by this and the teacher had to flee back into the school. After a few hours of our being intimidated one of the younger students looked out a window and said he believed the "daddy cow" was gone. The whole school was relieved to be able to go to the outhouses again.

One day a timber wolf came to visit. He stood a short distance away from the playground and quietly observed us - and we observed him. The teacher said he was a white dog but the older boys said "timber wolf" and we all knew they were right - the very long nose and the long bushy tail that did not wag did not signify a domesticated dog. Also our family dog had come over to the schoolyard and, with tail between his legs, was barking at the animal but keeping his distance.

Bertha Elizabeth Brennan
Kansas City, Kansas

The Hen That Came To School

Back in the early thirties, I was teaching in a one room rural school. Like all rural schools we had two outhouses located some distance apart near the line fence. In each outhouse was a flat wooden box that held a Montgomery Wards or Sears Roebuck catalog. The papers were used for toilet paper. Rolls of toilet tissue that we use today were unknown in that area at that time. Down the dirt road a short distance and across the road lived an old bachelor. I don't remember if he farmed much or not, but he had calves, dogs, cats and chickens. In the fall and spring when the chickens were laying well, we had one old hen that came to school each day and laid an egg on the catalog in the girls' toilet. Each day a girl would bring the egg to the schoolhouse where we carefully kept it till Friday. On Friday a couple of little girls would take our week's collection of eggs to the owner's house. He always thanked them and usually had some sort of treat for them. The girls sure looked forward to taking eggs to Mr. Oble every Friday.

Hazel Millenbruch
Home, Kansas

Permanent Residents

We have memories tied in with sounds and smells. When I smell lilacs or sweeping compound or honey, I get feelings that are associated with days in Happy Hollow school. One May morning, Teacher took the whole school, with the exception of two girls, on a hike and flower hunt along the creek that ran alongside of the school and wandered through our pasture. When we returned to the school with our little bits of violets and buffalo peas, the entire schoolroom was filled with the scent of lilacs. And on every desk was a bouquet and a little basket of candies and lilacs. (May baskets.)

Another time, because a swarm of bees had made our school walls their hiding place, two young men agreed with the School Board that they would "get rid of those bees for good." So they removed a bit of the foundation and ran a hose from their exhaust pipe under the schoolhouse and started up the motor on their '28 Model T Ford and blew the building partly off the foundation! It cost more to replace the building properly than it would have to hire exterminators. And the bees were still living there when we moved in 1932!

Lola Gilbert
Mohave Valley, Arizona

The Perfect Mousetrap

I went to a one room school in the late 1920s during the dark days of the deep depression. I had to walk five miles uphill, all the way knee deep in copperheads. I had to put stove pipes on my legs to keep from getting bit. When it got icy I would take one step forward and slide back two. So I had to walk backwards to make headway. Naw, naw, just kidding, just kidding.

School started in September 1928. It was surrounded by pastures, fields, meadows. Up front near the teacher's desk by the wall was the old pump organ, and a mouse came out and ran around there and scared the teacher quite often. Us boys thought it was funny to see her gasp and jerk. She was afraid the mice would chew on the bellows in the organ and ruin it. The school stood empty all last summer and the mice moved in in numbers.

I was a young schoolboy then and I had me a brand new Victor mouse trap at home that I gave a nickel or dime for and used at home. I offered to bring the trap to school the next day and catch the mice. The teacher was delighted.

So next morning I brought the trap to school. I baited it with a piece of toasted bacon and set it by the organ in plain sight of the classroom. After class took up and everything got quiet, I heard a lot of whispering and saw them pointing up front. A mouse was at the trap and started to gnaw at the bait. Everyone was holding their breath waiting for the trap to spring, which seemed to take forever. Tension was high, then suddenly "cur whak" and the trap sprang with a loud click. The girls and teacher shrieked and gasped. There was quite a show, but I thought it was funny. I took that mouse and chucked him outdoors. After that it was decided that I set the trap <u>after</u> school!

> Carl Kump
> Kansas City, Missouri

Dog Came To School

One day our little Beagle Dog came to school. It was very cold outdoors. I turned the dog in and it went to my 2 brothers' seats as they called him by name, "Trixie." We later wrote stories about him and studied about dogs later.

> Gertrude Rouggly
> Flat River, Missouri

Remembering Pets

My rural school days came to mind each time I see a collie dog or a spotted pony. Our dog, Laddie, sensed I needed someone to walk with me the mile to school during my first year. He took me to school each morning and returned to get me in the afternoons without being told. The teacher remarked they could see the dog coming in the distance before they saw me. A few years later I was sick and unable to walk so my Dad bought me a spotted pony for my brother and I to ride that year.

A few years ago I had the opportunity to sneak a peek into the vacant one-room schoolhouse. The room was not nearly as large as I remembered as a child.

> Wanda Wolf Bashford
> In Memory Of
> Chester Wolf
> Kidder, Missouri

Spooked The Old Gray Mare

My father decided we needed a horse to ride to school. So he went to an auction and bought an old (I mean "old") gray mare, she was swaybacked and all. My sister and I had never ridden much at all, especially double and bareback. So off we went, thinking how great.

All was fine until time to go home the first afternoon. There were 2 older neighbor boys that rode a small Shetland pony. They thought they would really have some fun with us on our big old gray mare. They came up running behind us and yelled like "Ride 'em Cowboy!" or something. That spooked our mare who started running, too! In not too great a distance my sister slid to one side and pulled me off and we both fell on the hard ground. We didn't ride the rest of the way home.

Theresa Bainbridge
La Salle, Colorado

(Editor's Note: "Molly" soon passed away, and the girls walked the rest of that year.)

Hickory Dickory Dock

By the late 1930s, one-room schools in Northwest Wisconsin were about to become things of the past.

I taught a year in one of them that left much to be desired. Not the least of the problems in the school was the over-abundance of families of mice. If I opened a desk drawer, one was almost certain to hop out. After the children left for the day, mice scurried up and down the aisles. I had no love for them!

One evening as I was in the cloak-room getting ready to leave for my boarding-place, one of the school board members dropped by.

I seized the opportunity to air my views concerning what needed to be done to improve the school. I was very vocal in my criticisms.

I was still complaining while I proceeded to pull on my woolen snowpants. As I did so, a mouse started climbing up my leg. I shrieked in fright and flung my leg forward. The mouse flew across the floor.

The Board member howled with laughter but managed to say, "You sure changed your tune!"

Credits go to the Board for setting out sufficient poison to eliminate the mice during Christmas vacation. What a relief!

Mary Gaylord
Balsam Lake, Wisconsin

Kind Teacher Eases Stings

Most teachers of country one room schools were real friends. They treated their students as family. I know that the one I had was more than a teacher.

I attended Peninsula country school back in 1928-29. It was one of the best times of my life, especially the time Mrs. Kathryn took Helen and me home with her to spend the night. We were going to help her grade test papers that night. That's what we were supposed to do. But, our teacher took us for a walk in the woods, along the shore of a creek. We did enjoy this. Our teacher was like a big sister to us. When we got back to the house, Helen and me decided to get rid of some wasp nests that were clinging to the eaves of the house. We started throwing clods of dirt at the wasps' nests. Boyee, did we ever get those wasps riled!

You guessed it! I was the one the wasps ganged up on. I got several stings. Sure they hurt! But Mrs. Kathryn dabbed each sting with kerosene. So I went ahead and enjoyed my overnight stay with the teacher and Helen - and checking those test papers.

I learned a big lesson as well. I learned to leave those wasps alone!

Marjorie Burd McGowin
Jerico Springs, Missouri

School Mascots

Most of the rural schools were not equipped with modern bathroom facilities, and one morning a little fellow came in from the outhouse with a little brown owl. He was cold and hungry, so we all took pity on him. It made a fine science lesson. The children shared cookie crumbs and bits of bread with him and the little owl was right at home.

He made no noise, but enjoyed sitting on the light fixtures where he could watch what was going on.

On weekends the boys took turns going to the schoolhouse to feed him and he became a nice friendly bird that would eat out of their hands.

In the spring we decided that he should be returned to his environment, since the school would be closed in May. He was returned to the outdoor facility where he was discovered.

Every morning for two weeks he was on the doorstep when I unlocked the door. I talked to him and fed him some goodies and he flew off. One day he was not there, but when I locked my car door, he sat on the fender. I petted him again and talked to him - and he flew away.

Madonna Storla
Postville, Iowa

Pecking Order

Just the mention of country school brings to mind a bevy of memories ranging from happy to the ridiculous.

Our new teacher was fresh out of high school normal training, not much older than the older kids and trying very hard to be dignified. She was very shy and prone to blushing crimson at the least provocation. As she boarded across the road from the school, her landlady brought lunch over on a tray each noon.

The first weeks of school were very warm and we took our lunch time outside. Teacher's lunch was fried chicken and all the trimmings.

The chickens from across the road made a habit of regularly patrolling the school yard, picking up discarded tidbits. A young rooster edged nearer and nearer to the porch, seemingly nonchalant as he paced back and forth cocking a curious stare at what we were eating. Suddenly he made a dive, a purposeful leap and zeroed in on teacher's tray. He snatched a chicken leg from the plate and tore for the road with all the other moochers in hot pursuit.

Needless to say she was stricken with embarrassment. The kids hooted and yelled their amusement while she turned all shades of scarlet. The others laughed but I did feel sorry for her!

Jean Kristiansen
Nashua, Iowa

Mickey And Minnie

Occasionally we caught mice in traps in the older country schools, but in one, we had two little mice which seemed to avoid our baited traps. We tried cheese, which should have enticed them, and even used peanut butter, to no avail.

After the noon recess, every class had a penmanship class. Of course it was quiet, and sure enough, our two little mice appeared. Two of the little girls named them Mickey and Minnie. Every pupil was quiet but watchful as the mice scampered down under the seats looking for crumbs of cookies or cake. When the noise of classes resumed, they disappeared.

This was a daily experience until one evening my husband came to get me from school. As we rode along, I realized we had an extra passenger. I asked him to stop quickly. I got out of the car, took off my coat and shook it. One of the little mice fell from my sleeve and scampered away.

The next morning I announced that one of our mice had been left on the roadside. Sure enough, during penmanship class, one lonely little mouse searched for tidbits under the rows of seats.

Madonna Storla
Postville, Iowa

Nature Class

In southeast Iowa, I taught a one-room school. There were 17 pupils, five grades.

Five of the pupils were from one family. They came by horse

and buggy.

One morning, they came late, but only sat in the buggy and gazed into the sky. I went to know the reason and other pupils followed. The driver, the eldest boy, said, "Pa said it was an eagle. We've watched it all the way."

A large bird was soaring in the distance. We were 2 miles from Skunk River. Eagles are rarely seen in Iowa. So we had a nature class that morning.

V.F. Brown
Niles, Michigan

Skunked

To make a little spending money and also to buy my clothes and books, I ran trap from the time I was about eight years old. One morning I caught a skunk in a rabbit trap, and it liberally sprayed my overall legs as I was trying to set it loose. As I was out in the open air, I didn't realize how bad it was and went on to school.

My desk was fairly close to the pot-bellied stove, and by mid-morning, the stench was obvious, even to me. When Teacher discovered the origin of the smell, she just decided to dismiss school for the rest of the day. I imagine she spent the rest of the day trying to get the room fumigated!

Edward W. Maxwell
Aurora, Missouri

(Editor's Note: Mr. Maxwell wrote this letter in 1979 for *Capper's Weekly*, and passed away in 1983. Permission to use parts of his letter was given by Mary Meyers, also of Aurora, Missouri.)

Pigs Got My Lunch

At 12 o'clock sharp Miss Vennie rang the lunch bell and the kids all grabbed their dinner pails and rushed outside, chattering all the while. I followed three older girls as they stopped under a big chestnut tree and began spreading out their lunches. My syrup bucket contained a biscuit and pork sausage sandwich, some fried potatoes, a boiled egg and an apple.

Before I had eaten half of my sandwich, here came an old sow and several hungry pigs, rooting their way toward us. One pig got my lunch pail hung over his nose and off he ran through the bushes towards the clay-banked creek where the cows were grazing, with me in hot pursuit! He wasn't about to get my lunch without a struggle!

Back at the chestnut tree the girls were laughing their heads off at the spectacle I was making. They, too, lost almost their entire lunch to the hungry sow and her family, but they seemed to find the whole thing more amusing than tragic. I managed to retrieve my apple, however, and they saved a few nuts.

Finally we trudged back to the schoolhouse and told our story to Miss Vennie, who insisted on dividing her ample lunch with us. We ended up with fried chicken, sliced tomatoes, and oatmeal cookies.

Mercedes Heyn
Ava, Missouri

(Editor's Note: Mercedes Heyn wrote this letter to *Capper's* in 1979, but passed away in 1986. This story is reprinted with the permission of Fred Heyn.)

Slithering Surprise

I was a 19-year-old green-horn, who didn't even know much about the state of Iowa. One day I was teaching a class (I had seven pupils in seven different grades), and a little boy shouted, "Miss Cloud! Look behind you!"

Much to my horror, I turned to see a huge bull snake trying to come up through the cold air register. It was waving around in the air almost as high as me. It was stuck and couldn't get through, its middle was too thick. The boys pulled up the register, and took it, with the snake, outside where they removed the snake and measured it. Six feet long! Everyone told me that they usually came in pairs and where there was one the other one would be around looking for its mate. I had nightmares for several nights, and was afraid to put my feet under the teacher's desk, or go into the cloakroom for days, but we didn't see any more snakes.

Alice R. Mason
Toledo, Iowa

Whooo's In The Stove?

One bitter cold morning when I arrived at my little one room schoolhouse to make the fire in my big old cast-iron stove, I heard a noise inside the stove. It sounded like something scratching. My first thought was rats. I just didn't know what to do, but I had to get that fire started so I opened the door of the stove a crack, and out flew a big old owl.

It flew up on the stovepipe that went across the room. I couldn't reach it, or I should say I was too big a coward to get near the thing, so I just let it sit, hoping it would fly out the door.

I went in the old coal shed and got cobs and coal to get the fire going. After a bit the pipes got hot and the poor old thing got hot feet and flew to the back of the recitation bench.

About that time the children started to arrive and I asked them what I should do, as I knew they had more experience with owls than I ever had. They really encouraged me by saying, "Don't go near it or it will pluck out your eyes."

After a time another little boy arrived and without saying much came to my rescue and went up behind the bench and grabbed the thing and carried it out. Poor owl was more frightened than I was, I'm sure, after the experience he had.

I never will forget it. I could have hugged that little boy for coming to the rescue of a frightened teacher.

Hester Arentson
Harlan, Iowa

A Bull In The Schoolyard

It was my first year of teaching and it was in a one room country school, located down the lane of a farm where in one of the grazing fields the farmer occasionally had cattle.

MY FOLKS AND THE ONE-ROOM SCHOOLHOUSE

As I was a town-raised girl, I was apprehensive of the cattle but was assured that there would be no cattle in the field during school hours. I accepted this, but with much misgiving in my mind.

Each morning as I went down the lane, I carefully looked around the field before scurrying up to the schoolhouse. Only once in awhile would I see a few cattle down in the far corner grazing contentedly; paying no attention to me so I timidly but quickly got to the school and inside giving a sigh of relief.

We always had our recess outside, weather permitting, but this one morning one of the boys came to me and said, "Teacher, I don't think we had better go outside for recess today."

"Why not?" I asked, and Jim said, "Well, my Dad's bull is out in the field." I immediately agreed that we shouldn't go out but stay in and play some indoor games instead for a change.

Naturally the inevitable happened, nature called and one of the boys asked permission to leave the room. We looked out the window but didn't see our friend, so I agreed, but cautioned him to look carefully and if he saw him to not take any chances and run back inside.

Jim started around the side of our building and so did the bull. Both started for the school door and Jim got there in time for us to close and fasten the door. There were two doors on the full length porch which were only fastened with a latch and quite unstable from long usage, so we began to pile desks in front of each door as we could hear our friend prancing and bellowing back and forth out on that porch, just as our boy was prancing very uncomfortably inside, back and forth.

There we were, twenty-five children and one teacher, all frightened wondering what was going to happen next. We decided to quiet down and maybe he would forget about us and go away. Finally he deigned to jump down and start eating again.

It came time for dismissal and a decision had to be made. We couldn't stay there all night, with children six to fourteen years old. What were we to do?

Finally the bull decided to cooperate and ambled down to the far corner of the field. Jim came to me and said, "Teacher, the bull knows me and I think I can slip out of the door and run up and get my Dad to come down and take him out of the field for us." Jim was successful and we all got ready to go home.

You can believe me that teacher didn't stay to sweep the floor that night, but started walking home with the children.

It was the first time I had every heard of a bull trying to go to school!

Helen Sexton
Arlington, Texas

(Editor's Note: Helen Sexton wrote this story in 1979 for *Capper's*, but passed away in 1983. Permission to use this story was given by Dorothy Sexton.)

Revenge Is Well-Cooked

The one-room school teacher often received a special initiation at the new school.

This young teacher from the east was very thrilled to get a school in an old, almost deserted western mining camp. The school boasted 11 pupils, and everyone knew everyone else in camp.

The third day of school the teacher opened the top drawer of her desk and a big, fat wharf rat jumped out in her lap. For the next few minutes everyone played a game of "find the rat."

The game ended when someone dealt the rat a fatal blow with the iron poker, and school was again in normal session. The teacher had asked a few casual questions and made a few shrewd deductions of her own about how that live rat just happened to be in her tightly-closed desk drawer.

At recess time she headed for the girls' room in the trees out back. But she went right on past it, and came to a house where a bachelor lived. He was in the habit of leaving a kettle of food cooking on the big cast iron stove so he would have a meal ready when he returned from work. This day when he returned from work he added some fuel to the smoldering coals. He washed up and moved the coffee pot to the front of the stove, and set the table and took his plate to the stove for his hot supper.

He took the lid off the kettle and there, right on top, was a well-cooked wharf rat.

After that the little tender-footed teacher from the east never did find another rat in her desk.

Ola M. Hughes
Pueblo, Colorado

CHAPTER 8: A Tale For All Seasons

No Snow Days

I don't recall having snow days off while attending a one-room school. Of course, there were no school bus routes then, either. Every family provided their own transportation. Bad weather meant putting on the chains and plowing through. If some couldn't make it in the farm truck, those students stayed home, but the school went on. The teacher probably had it worst, having to drive out all the way from town.

Smell is the sense most evocative of memories. My nose certainly remembers the distinctive singed odor of mittens steaming dry, close to the hot stove.

                        Carol Darnell
                        Columbia, Missouri

Seasonal Smells

I was born on a Nebraska farm in 1907. That must have been before the word deodorant was in the dictionary.

I attended a one room country school where over forty people had to breathe the same air for eight hours.

In snowy wet weather our clothes would be wet by the time we walked to school. We would dry our wet clothes standing near the old coal heater. We didn't have enough clothes to change every day or have the facilities to take baths. Some of the older boys ran their trap line on the way to school, and sometimes caught a skunk or two.

Prying our lid off our syrup pail dinner bucket, we got another whiff of stale air from the food in that air tight container. I carried that old bucket for eight years.

Sometimes just to get a breath of fresh air we held up our hand with one finger extended, a nod from the teacher gave us permission to go to the outhouse. We didn't tarry long as the smell of the outhouse would almost peel the skin off the inside of your nose.

Summer time at home meant cow piles and old black chicken manure that got between your bare toes. Cleaning them, your fingers were involved.

Butchering time always brought its share of smells. It was my job to help clean the intestines of the hogs for sausage stuffing. They had to be emptied, turned wrong side out and scraped and soaked. Cleaning chickens you had to remove those wet, smelly feathers that stuck to your fingers and made you gag.

Making soap you had to stir the hot grease and lye in an old iron kettle over an open fire. It would tickle your nose and take your breath away. Then there was the smoke from the fire.

There were good smells, good times, friendship and the love of your family. But that is another story.

Pearl Shockley
Owensville, Missouri

Ditch Provides Shelter

I will never forget one time when I was going to a country school and one fall we pupils were busy studying when a neighbor man barged into the room and said "Teacher help me get all of these pupils out in the side ditch. I want all of you to come and lay down where I tell you to because there is a tornado coming." I will never forget to my dying day how the wind tugged at my clothing as I lay there. Of course all of us were frightened and crying, but it passed over pretty soon, and as we got up this man showed us where the telephone poles had pieces of straw stuck in the poles like nails. Just about $1/2$ mile south of the schoolhouse the storm had destroyed some of the farm buildings, so we were very thankful for that man.

I don't know if it was that same winter or not, but we lived 3/4 mile from the school and one morning which was very unusual Dad said, "I am taking you to school in the sled." This may be hard for you to believe but there were huge snow banks and the horses walked on top of the banks. The snow was so hard with a very thick crust on top.

Alice Jenkins
Lamoni, Iowa

Kerosene Was The Cure

During the Armistice Day Snowstorm in 1940 my sister and I started walking to school. We had to walk into the north wind when we left our lane. The wind and snow from the blizzard was so severe I told my sister I couldn't go any further. A pheasant dropped at our feet so we turned around and went home. If we had gotten to school the teacher would not have been able to get there.

With all the clothes we wore, scarves over our faces, long underwear, and long stockings we had frostbitten feet in the winter.

Some methods we used to alleviate the pains was to sponge our feet with kerosene and going barefoot in the snow. We just got cold feet from this.

Olga (Huntemann) Feyerherm
West Point, Nebraska

Too Close For Comfort

My story goes back to sixth grade. It was a nice sunny day in September. We were having History class in the front of the room. This was about 2:30 in the afternoon. My younger brother had just returned from the outside toilet. He came and whispered in my ear that the sky looked funny. I sensed that he was frightened. I told our teacher, Miss Jones, and she immediately went to check the sky. Upon her return, she told the whole school to follow her out of doors. When we all got out of the school, she told us to cross the road and lie down in the ditch. We all did - and it wasn't long before we heard a terrible roaring wind. The tornado was passing through a field about 200 feet to the south. This tornado left a path of destruction for many miles.

Thanks to my 6-year-old brother and a very caring teacher, no harm came to us.

Marjorie Goodman
Cedar Rapids, Iowa

Slippery When Wet

The falling rain froze on the ground that March, which marked the near end of my first year in our one room country schoolhouse.

My father got out the old wagon and hitched up the big plow horses to it to take us the mile that we usually walked to school each morning. My older sister and two brothers were ready to go as my mother buttoned me into my coat. "Now be careful," she said, "that's ice out there."

I took a step out the kitchen door and promptly landed on my behind. Everyone laughingly helped me up and I tried again, only to have the same thing happen. Puzzled, I attempted to get up by myself but couldn't. My parents decided to let the matter go at that; and I stayed home for the day, my brothers and sister riding off high up in the wagon behind the horses and my father.

I watched them go, still not really understanding what ice was, but only that they knew how to deal with it better than I. It took my feet until the next year to figure it all out.

Barbara Queen
Rosemead, California

From Dawn To Dust

I was teaching in a one room school back in the dirty thirties. I remember one day when the dust in the air was so thick that it was almost as dark as night. It was so dark in the schoolhouse that we could not have classes or do any studying. I tried to spend the time reading to the pupils. The school was built of limestone rock so the window sills were wide enough for a seat. I tried to sit in a window and read, but that was impossible. It was too dark, so I decided to dismiss school. I was driving my father's Model A Ford to school so I decided to take the children all home because I was afraid some of them would get lost.

After taking several children home, I went to the last home where two little girls lived. They asked me to come in. The women of the neighborhood were having an all-day quilting bee at this home. They were quilting in spite of the darkness. They slid a large table under the quilt which was in a quilting frame. Then they placed a kerosene lamp on the middle of the quilt and continued quilting. The table made a firm foundation for the lamp.

We had more dark days, but that was the worst I remember.
Hazel Millenbruch
Home, Kansas

High Water Worries

One year, on the Friday afternoon before Christmas, we had our little Christmas party and gift exchange, and the teacher dismissed us early. It had been raining for several days and it was very cold. My parents came to pick us up, but, because we had been dismissed early, they missed us. The creeks were up. We managed to get across the first two small ones, but when we got to the last one, the "big" one, it was knee-deep and rolling swiftly with big chunks of ice and other debris. We could not find a good place to cross, so decided we may as well try to cross in our usual place. My big sister and the biggest neighbor girl waded across, taking one of us smaller ones by the hand, until they got us all safely through. Our clothes were frozen by the time we got to the house. My parents were frantic, and very relieved that we were safe. We could have easily been swept away and drowned. Fortunately, we did not even get sick from the exposure.

MY FOLKS AND THE ONE-ROOM SCHOOLHOUSE

After that, my father cut down a huge tree that reached from one bank to the other, chiseled off the top side to make it flat, put a hand rail on it, and built steps on one end, so that we had a foot bridge. He did not want that to happen again.

Eileen Grube
Gerald, Missouri

Alcohol As Antifreeze

I drove my old 1920 touring car until the snow banks were higher than it and the slightest wind would fill the narrow path shoveled out by manpower every day. No heater, but my father had fixed a pipe so the exhaust would run under the car under my feet and there were icing glass and leather sidecurtains. Alcohol in the radiator for an anti-freeze boiled away often to a reduced strength as I drove those seven miles to school. On the coldest days when I arrived I would turn a little petcock under the car and drain the contents of the radiator into a pail which I would set behind the stove in the schoolhouse. There were times when it turned a thick greenish mush before night, though it had been drained boiling hot from the radiator. After school, I would dash out, start the car, race in and pour the pail of water-alcohol mixture in the radiator, then wait with the car running to keep it from freezing in the radiator. I was young and strong, but sometimes I could not turn the crank long enough to start it and the big boys would take turns doing it.

At last there came a day when I could no longer get through and I remember it took three days with a big crew of men shoveling to cover the seven miles. This was in Iowa, close to the Minnesota border.

Hazel Hoyt Markovetz
Urbandale, Iowa

School Threatened By Raging Waters

One thing that stands out in my memory is the time I was teaching in a school located in the bottom of a canyon. I boarded with a family one-half mile away. A dark cloud rolled in from the north early one morning. I ran most of the way down that long hill and got to school just before the rain hit. I could hear the water raging down the canyon, it kept getting higher and higher. It got up to the top of the fencepost, the barn was standing in a foot of water. Water came almost to the schoolhouse.

There being no telephone I had no way of knowing if any of the pupils had started to school. I couldn't get across the draw. Finally a little after noon a few pupils walked in wearing hip waders. Needless to say, there wasn't much school that day.

Lorraine Priddy
Stratton, Nebraska

Snowbound Slumber Party

The blizzard that we experienced on March 11, 1977, reminded my wife of an experience that we had in a storm fifty years ago. I was a country schoolteacher and school bus driver. My bus was a 1918 Model T Ford, quite a car at the time. It had a top that could be put up and side curtains that could be put in place in stormy weather.

On this memorable day in March 1925, I had four children with me. The weather being very threatening, no more of the fifteen pupils that usually attended showed up. As the morning wore on the storm intensified and I decided to dismiss school and head home with my four pupils.

We ate our lunches before starting and I bundled my pupils into the Model T with robes and quilts that I always carried.

The Model T started all right but before we had traveled one-half mile the blizzard had intensified to the extent that the blowing snow whipped up under the hood, wetting the motor and the electrical wires and the motor died. The only thing to do was walk back to the schoolhouse and wait out the storm or the arrival of possible help.

I lined the children up in a row, covered them completely with the quilts from the car, and led them back to the schoolhouse. I carried plenty of coal in from the coal house to last the rest of the day and possibly the night. We moved four long benches into a square around the stove.

We sang songs and played games to pass the time. If I remember right we had three sandwiches left in our five lunch pails, which we made do for supper.

Not long after daylight the next morning, we saw a man ride into the schoolyard on a horse. It was the father of the Teel children. He had started out at daylight to try to find us. He had become lost in the storm trying to find his way to the schoolhouse, just two miles from his home. He was aimlessly drifting in the storm, when he accidentally saw the schoolhouse, which he was about to pass.

This is just one of the harrowing experiences my wife and I went through during my twenty years as a country school teacher in Kit Carson County, Colorado.

J. Carl Harrison
Vona, Colorado

(Editor's Note: This story was submitted to *Capper's* in 1979, and Mr. Harrison graciously agreed to let us use it now.)

School Stood While Prairie Burned

One year as my Mother taught in the one-room school, fires broke out everywhere. The children became frightened and excited. They couldn't study.

It seems it was a very dry year. The grass was tall, and the wires of the cattle fences would rub together when the wind blew and would produce sparks that set the prairie on fire.

The school stood, the fires didn't get to it.

Pauline Fecht
Syracuse, Kansas

Hip-Deep In Snow

I not only attended a one-room school, but I taught in the same one for the handsome wages of $50 per month, which was good wages in Nebraska in the "Dirty Thirties."

One of my memories is of a big snow, several feet deep, accompanied by the usual bitter cold wind. When it was time for me to walk the mile to school, my mother insisted that my older brother accompany me to help build the fire in the coal heater and carry drinking water from the neighboring farm-stead.

With the wind blowing, the snow developed a thick crust on top. It would support my 98 pounds, but would break under my 6 foot brother's weight. He floundered hip-deep in the snow while I walked on top, so by the time we reached the schoolhouse he was exhausted and had to rest while I built the fire, carried water and scooped paths to the outdoor "sanitary facilities!"

Leola Bowers
Ft. Collins, Colorado

Vivid Memories

One memory still vivid in my mind is the dust storms. We would see a dust storm rolling in. We would get loaded and the bus would go up a hill to the first place about 3/4 mile from the school. This family would get out near the house and then the driver would park the bus beside a quonset and usually set there for about an hour. It would be so black one could not see their hand a few inches in front of their face. After an hour or so the driver would start, as usually one could see a little. Everyone on the bus would watch and when and if you saw a fencepost they would tell the driver, helping keep the bus on the right tract. Eventually we would get everyone delivered. When we got off the bus at our house, at least four of us, we held hands and walked to the house. Mama would always set the lamp by a window and they always had the yard gate open.

Another time it was a cold frosty morning. A creek (dry most of the time) was just north of the school. A bridge was over the creek as that was the deepest part. A family lived about 1/2 mile up the creek. One morning one of the boys had a cold so the teacher sent him home to get his own drinking cup. In our country school we took a cream can full of water each morning and everyone drank out of the same dipper.

Anyway, Hugh started home and as he went under the bridge, he got the "bright" idea to stick his tongue on a steel pilling. Of course his tongue got stuck and he didn't think or know to blow his breath to loosen his tongue, he just pulled it off and took all the skin off his tongue. Needless to say, he didn't come back to school. At noon the teacher sent his brother home to see why.

Mildred O. Jones Waldren
Tribune, Kansas

Rainy Revenge

One spring lightning struck our brick country schoolhouse; tearing out one corner of the building and making it unsafe to continue classes in it.

So the school board decided to pitch a tent in the schoolyard to continue having school until a new native stone schoolhouse could be built.

We had our air conditioned classroom. We could roll up the sides of the tent each day for fresh air and to let the daylight in. And if the air was hot outside we had a hot classroom, if it was cold outside we would have a cold classroom.

Our tent was cloth-coated with something to make it weatherproof. All we had to do to make it leak during a rain was scratch a spot with our fingernails. Some of us not-so-perfect students scratched places over the teacher's desk and chair, he got a free shower when it rained. (Editor's Note: He was not referred to as a particularly devoted or pleasant teacher.)

I had a desk on the outside row of seats, and there was a ground squirrel hole close by my desk. Every day I watched the little squirrel do its thing. I watched it for long periods of time. It wasn't afraid of us kids. I had a lesson every day in nature and science, but didn't get a grade for it.

Now I tell my grandkids about when I went to school in a tent and they can't imagine such a thing.

Tiny Hensley
Independence, Kansas

Winter Wonderland

After a howling blizzard during the night,

A TALE FOR ALL SEASONS

The snow looked so beautiful and white
We couldn't use the kitchen door for the snow,
Where the wind had piled and packed it so.

The snow was drifted in swirls and waves
With peaks, valleys, tunnels and caves
Reminding me of my childhood days
When winter storms came in a similar way.

We walked a mile to attend our school
And were taught to live by the "Golden Rule."
We studied our lessons and recited them well
Arithmetic, reading, writing and learned to spell.

All eight grades by one teacher were taught
In the one room country school our lunches we brought
Around the big pot belly stove we moved our seats
Where we could warm our bodies and feet.

On Fridays we had poems to recite,
Also cyphered long or short arithmetic division on the blackboard
Subtraction, addition, geography, naming states and capitals,
A very exciting fun time.

We also studied language, spelling and art
We opened each morning school singing a song
On cold winter days we played games inside
We all wrapped up good and took dinners along.

A neighbor would hitch a team to a bob sled,
With straw, heated rocks and sideboards on the bed.
The farmer would whistle as he drove along
While sleigh bells would jingle a song.
Children had been bundled up good and warm,
And were delivered to their own family farm.
       Ruth Jincks
       Bethany, Missouri

Teacher Was Prepared

On a perfectly clear day we could look to the northwest and see a black boiling cloud rising from the horizon. It looked very much like heavy smoke from a freight train. But our teacher was prepared. We all kept a small box of Rosebud salve and a white mens' handkerchief in our desks. The teacher would instruct us to put the salve around our nostrils and helped to tie the handkerchief around our faces. Then we would lay our heads on our arms on our desks.

Glenna Turner
Hardesty, Oklahoma

Songs Ease Storm

A few minutes before "take-up" time one morning, I noticed a startling change in sky and air. It meant a storm was about to strike. I called the children inside and got them settled before the thunder bellowed and the lightning zig-zagged. The wind whipped leaves, tumbleweeds and limbs against our sturdy old frame building. It became dark as rain poured as if from firehoses against the windows. The children were scared and cried as they clung to me. I consoled them as best I knew. I passed out our ragged songbooks and suggested we sing. The organ wheezed and squeaked as I accompanied. We sang "America," "Yankee Doodle," "Old MacDonald Had A Farm," and others. Still the storm thundered and poured. Marlin, a long-legged sixth grader, requested page sixty-three. It was "God Be With You Till We Meet Again." He was scared. We sang his choice and more. Suddenly the storm subsided as Kansas thunderstorms sometimes do. The day became bright and we began our Readin', 'Ritin' and 'Rithmetic.

Mary Worley
Azalea, Oregon

CHAPTER 9: Special Days

Physical Education Of The Natural Sort

Living one and a half miles from our one-room school, I was usually driven there by a family member, except in the spring when the weather was more pleasant. Then, after school several of us would walk back home together, as far as our mutual paths went. Because of the dangers of a highway that I had to follow for half the route, I was only occasionally allowed to ride my bike.

The children I really envied were those who had horses to ride to school. A barn was in the corner of the school grounds. At noon we'd all go and help the owner feed and water the animal, and of course add a bit of petting and patting to reassure our visitor.

The barn, when unoccupied, was also a source of daring fun - almost as breathless as the challenge of clambering up the door and jumping off the smaller coal shed roof (into a sandpile, left from the more conventional jumping events of the annual county track meet). The wooden fencing dividing the barn's interior into two stalls served as a test of "how big are you?"

One by one we'd climb to the top post, stand erect for a moment, precariously in balance like a circus performer, and then leap off while reaching for the overhead rafters. If we could grab them and pull ourselves up onto the rafter floor of the hayloft, we had a high haven secure from the pesky little kids who couldn't possible imitate our feat.

In those simpler days before liability insurance and organized school sports, we didn't miss expensive gymnastic equipment or karate lessons to build sturdy limbs and confident physical prowess. We just did physical exercise the natural way.

       Carol Darnell
       Columbia, Missouri

Didn't Miss A Day

Our family lived on a farm about a mile from a one-room schoolhouse. When I was five years old the teacher, who was boarding at our home, invited me to walk along and visit school on opening day. I was completely entranced - didn't miss a day the whole school term.

Some of our recess and noon extra minutes were fun time for all. The favorites were games: softball, pump pump pull away, last couple out, steal the stick, dare base, and baseball. For quieter fun times - jump the rope, hopskotch and storytelling or oral reading.

When the weather was too cold for outdoor fun we did chalkboard games, guess riddles, spelling bees and geography trivia. Blind Man's Bluff was fun to the younger students. When spring time arrived the boys would dig up a few feet of sod and use it for practicing the high jump, broad jump and longest-distance running jump. Some did quite well! We were taught, "you're not likely to achieve anything of lasting value in life if you never take a chance and try!"

       Matilda (Winters) Cardin
       Englewood, Colorado

Games At Point School

We walked to the one-room school, Point School, when I had Mrs. Hazel Hieronymus for my teacher all eight years. At school we played circle games like two-deep, fox and geese, and some ball, but the most fun was "Andy-over" - throwing the ball over the schoolhouse with a team on each side. If one side caught the ball, they came around trying to tag someone to capture them for their side, and we would run fast to get over to the other side without getting caught!

Elizabeth Hardy
Jacksonville, Illinois

Countless Opportunities

The first two years we attended the one-room school the yard had only a sturdy teeter totter. There was not even a swing. Some time during the summer between our last two years, some of the neighbor farmers added a pole with a basketball backboard and hoop. We often used to shoot goals, but we never played the game. Very likely, no one knew the rules of the game and the rough grass was not very suitable for a court.

We played various games, some acquired from previous students, some we invented. Often the entire school participated together, notwithstanding a broad range of ages and abilities.

Steal the Sheep required two teams. A short stick (the sheep) was leaned from the porch floor to the ground. One team guarded it while the other attempted to sneak in and knock it down, then run so as not to get caught. Each member caught became a member of the rival team.

Ball Bouncing. This required no teams. All played together. One person threw the ball high against the building wall, calling a person's name. He or she was to catch it before it touched the ground or on the first bounce. This gave the younger ones a better chance.

Marbles. Every spring marbles was a popular game, continuing over several weeks. The children brought marbles from home. Playing "for keeps" was not allowed.

Jumping rope, individually or with others, was always popular.

Mumble-the-peg was a pocket knife game always popular

with farm boys who often carried knives.

Baseball was played frequently, using a baseball I had made from a piece of a rubber heel wrapped with thread I had accumulated over a year or more, ripped from the tops of dad's work sox. The cover was cut from leather uppers from discarded shoes. The bat was a tree branch. There were not enough pupils for two teams, so we played Work-up. Essential positions were assigned: pitcher, catcher, batter, basemen and a pig-tailer (beyond the pitcher). After an out was made, or a run, each person moved up a position, as pitcher to catcher, etc. This way everyone had the opportunity to play often, even though there were not two teams. An out, by the way, was called when a ball was thrown in front of a runner, between him and the base toward which he was running.

Edna Easter
Independence, Missouri

Sun Beat Us Home

I taught in one room school from 1919 to 1923. It was on the prairies of Colorado. There were about 20 pupils in the school from first grade through eighth.

Occasionally on weekends we would push the desks along the wall and on Saturday evenings have square dances. A lady in the community played the organ and one of the men the fiddle. There was a small charge, twenty five cents I believe, which we would use to buy a book or something for the school. Ladies in the community furnished lunch. Often times the sun was coming up before we left to go home.

Katherine Schwynoch
Salem, Oregon

Reciting At School Programs

About fifty years ago, the night of the programs at the one room country school was a big event. The school I attended had a stage at the front of the room with heavy wine colored curtains to be pulled by hand for the plays and pieces the children of the school would perform.

Most of the parents came to watch the children. At this time the parents were all married and no step-parents.

Some of the pieces the children said I remember. The one my little sister recited I remember the best:

"Thanksgiving is coming
The time is drawing near,
When mamma bakes pies
And daddy hunts deer.
We will have turkey
And many things more,
I hope I don't eat
Til my tummy gets sore." (She rubbed her tummy, rolled her eyes and ran off the stage - everyone clapping and laughing.)

Betty Jane Atkinson
Fair Grove, Missouri

Special Days

After thirty-one years of classroom teaching, then retiring from the profession, I recall my first and one of my most pleasurable experiences of fifty-two years ago. It was in a one-room rural school. It really seems as if it were only yesterday that it took place as I sit here reminiscing.

In October we studied about Columbus, and made stories and decorations as we read his history.

On November 11, we stopped everything for a few minutes of meditation and silent prayer, to remember the soldiers who gave their lives and fought during World War I. We had this memorial at 11 a.m. because that was the time the Armistice was signed. It was called Armistice Day, but is now called Veterans' Day. We made decorations for this day and for Thanksgiving Day later in the month.

In November we also had a box supper and school program with the participation of the children. Each lady who attended brought a decorated box to the supper. In this box she had some delicious food. After the program, the boxes were auctioned and the highest bidder of each box had the privilege of eating that food with the lady who owned the box. This was an exciting occasion for everyone concerned. Usually the gentleman did not know whose box he bid on, unless someone cheated. The proceeds from the boxes were used for Christmas treats of candy, nuts and fruit.

At these night programs we had no electric lights. Gasoline lanterns were brought by several people and these were hung from the ceiling.

One thing indelibly stamped on my mind during this December, 1941, was what happened on December 7, when the Japanese bombed Pearl Harbor in Hawaii and World War II began. The next morning, on Monday, I can still visualize the picture at school, with the students and me gathered around our "Warm Morning" heating stove. We were quite concerned about our soldier friends and relatives.

In February we enjoyed a lovely Valentine Party. Each child and I had put our valentines to be given to others in a large box that I had decorated. We played some quiet games like Bingo, checkers and dominoes, as we did on cold days when we could not play outside. The older children passed the valentines. Each one was anxious to see his own and to see who gave him one. Refreshments of cookies and hot chocolate were served at the close of the party just before we went home.

Sibyl Webb
Hinton, Oklahoma

Memorization Helped In Regular Class

I began my career as a teacher in a one room school in the early forties. I was fresh out of high school where Normal Training was taught, which meant you spent your last two years of high school cramming all the techniques needed for teaching as well as the subject matter to be taught into a two-year program.

Every December the student body would put on a Christmas

program. The teacher would purchase books in which were written Christmas plays and poems. Then parts were assigned and each student had to memorize their character's speaking part in the short plays plus Christmas songs. The younger students would receive poems and recitations to memorize. More often than not each student would be in several plays and have speaking parts in them as well. I always felt this was very good for their minds. The memorization helped train their minds to retain facts taught in their regular classes. At the close of the hour-long program Santa would appear and pass out gifts that the teacher had for each student as well as the gifts the students gave each other. To ensure each student receiving one gift, names were drawn which often led to moans as a boy would draw a girl's name from the hat or a girl drawing a boy's name. Everyone was remembered this way. The teacher gave a gift to each child and received a gift from each child. The gifts given were about $1.00 in value and the teacher received a lot of bath powder, stationery and the like.

Teaching was a very rewarding experience as by teaching all eight grades a teacher could observe children of all ages growing in knowledge and developing social skills from their contact with children of various ages.

Delores Utecht
Wayne, Nebraska

Holiday Sparks Creativity

Those of us who attended a one room country school often speak of our relationship as being like one big happy family, forgetting that discord also occurs in families. As the only beginner I was an easy target for some of the bigger kids to "pick on" during recess. As in a biological family, one of the older girls took on the role of my protector and taught me the coping techniques that I would use throughout my life when dealing with bullies and other nasty types.

We country grade school children always looked forward to our annual Halloween party. During the previous week we'd spend our free moments cutting out silhouettes of jack-o-lanterns and cats for window decorations. We'd save the scraps of orange and black construction paper to make long chains that were hung from corner to corner of the ceiling.

The main event at our party was the costume contest. Because no one purchased ready-made costumes, we were very creative with sheets, old clothes, pillows, etc. Even our masks were homemade from paper sacks using dried corn silk as hair or beards.

Roasting marshmallows and bobbing for apples were two traditional activities at our parties.

The Halloween party was a festive time that brought out the spirit of creativity!

Helen Van Zante Boertje
Pella, Iowa

The Deacon's Honeymoon

It was the year 1925-26 that I was the only girl in the 8th grade in our school, District 52, Brantford Township, Washington County Kansas.

Our teacher, a local young lady, well-known and respected in the area, together with other young people came onto the idea of presenting a community play. Several plays were reviewed and finally a 3-act play, "The Deacon's Honeymoon" was chosen. It would be put on right there in our schoolhouse.

All interested participants met to discuss the play and decide on parts. My older sister, also a teacher in a neighboring school, was to be one of the participants, and of course my curiosity was beyond bounds as to which part she would play. The part of "deacon" was to be played by a prominent unmarried farmer and stockman. Several other prominent young farmers or farm hands also had parts. Some were to be paired off romantically, my sister was one of those, which I found interesting. Our teacher, because of her shorter stature, was designated to be a servant girl, handy whenever errands of a sudden nature needed tending to. All in all about a dozen various actors took part.

SPECIAL DAYS

Practices were held regularly at the schoolhouse, rides were pooled, others walked to practices across the fields.

Curtains were borrowed from a larger school, for other programs we had used sheets; a hallway ran most of the way along the east side of the schoolhouse, this was curtained-off the very day of the performance into two dressing rooms, one for ladies, one for men. Windows of this were rubbed over on the inside with Bon-Ami for privacy. People were barred from entering through the hallway so another entryway had to be provided. The southwest window of the main schoolroom was removed and ramps, like a stile, were built up and over where the window had been taken out. A heavy canvas was hung as a curtain to keep out the cold and yet allow entry. Everyone who came somehow managed this way of entry. The big stove that ordinarily stood in the middle of the schoolroom was moved to the back of the room with pipes reset so it could be used. Gas lamps and lanterns provided lights. Gas lanterns served as footlights. These were set on several uniformly-sawed measures of a large log. Galvanized tin was securely fastened to each log around the back sides of each lantern, thus directing the lighting onto the stage which had been constructed of bridge planks laid across sturdy sawhorses.

In readiness for the play, excessive use was made of "make-up" and even burnt cork. Some of the ladies borrowed wigs of anyone, even of a slight acquaintance, that had a wig.

An enormous crowd gathered on this perfect evening in March with no wind, no sleet, no snow. Extra seating had been provided by way of planks set on sturdy bases. The play went off "without a hitch," everyone playing their part well, to the enjoyment of all who came.

We pupils of the regular school had a part between acts as we lined up for a number in song, "The Storybook Ball." I recall being Old Mother Hubbard, my little sister was Little Miss Muffet, one brother may have been Humpty Dumpty, while a younger brother may have been Little Jack Horner.

Between the other two acts there was a brother-sister duet

number, with encore. One song they sang was popular that year and was entitled, "I'm Going to Let the Bumblebee Buzz."

Following the program there was an auction of boxes for a box supper. Ladies from the play and other ladies of the community brought beautifully decorated boxes filled with sandwiches and other goodies. The young men of the community bought these boxes. Each young man partook of the food with the lady whose box he had successfully bid on. Plates of food were also sold to others in the audience.

Of course, the following day there again was activity at the schoolhouse as all evidence of the eventful night was cleared away.

By Monday morning school was back in session as usual. (Footnote: In time, our schoolteacher married the prominent farmer who played the part of "deacon.")

Astrid Kisby
Clifton, Kansas

Remembers Poem After Many Years

I remember at Christmas time that year, I was given a part in the Christmas program. A poem that goes like this:

"I wish I had a telephone with golden wires unfurled,
Long enough and strong enough to reach around the world,
I'd call up everybody around the world and say,
A very Merry Christmas
To you this Christmas Day."

I'm 74 years old now, but I've never forgotten this poem.

Mildred Deason
Mound City, Kansas

Murder In The Night

I remember a poem I did at one occasion:
"The night was dark and dreary,
And a storm was drawing night

Lightning flash across the sky.
But see from out a lonely wood
There comes a vengeful man
A blood-stained club is firmly
Grasped within his strong right hand.
The club is raised
It falls with a sickening thud,
And there on the cold damp ground
Lays murdered
A potato bug!"
Thelma Clements
Portland, Oregon

Curriculum Toss-Up

In the 1920's I taught in Missouri in a one-room country school where all grades, one through eight, were in one room, except one year you taught fifth and seventh and the next year sixth and eighth. Some children might have sixth before fifth and eighth before seventh. However, the curriculum was arranged so it didn't make any difference.
Claracy Ingels
Roswell, New Mexico

Apple Pie Anguish

School started in September and we got out in April. Once we had a pie supper, and Mother made me an apple pie. A little boy in my class (there were seven in first grade) bought my box for 25¢. I cried. I was afraid to eat with him and didn't!
Helen Jacobs
Clarence, Missouri

The Demise Of The Country School

Since I was born March 24, 1910, almost nothing is now the same. There were one room country schools everywhere and most towns had a high school. Then, dusty and muddy roads were everywhere. The older women's skirts almost swept the floor. The games at school were Kick the Bucket, Work Up, (a brand of baseball), Fox and Geese, Andy Over, marbles and horseshoes, coasting parties, skating parties and visits to the old swimming hole. On the farm, horses still pulled the wagon, buggy and plow.

Before long the airplane started to make its mark. The Model T became the king of the road. As they made better cars and built better roads it hastened the one room school and small town demise. In the countryside now there is one house where there used to be eight.

William Woodward
Plevna, Missouri

Barefoot Teacher

I do remember very well teaching in a one room school in mid-Missouri during World War II.

Gasoline was rationed, so I walked 3 miles each way to and from school. Shoes were also rationed, therefore I wore heavy boots so they would last the allotted time until another shoe stamp was due.

I recall one September noon hour when an exciting softball game was in progress. I had kicked off my shoes to increase my speed if I should hit a ball. As I was standing on first base, a tall, well dressed, city looking, business-like salesman came walking straight toward first base. He asked where he might find the teacher and I vowed she wasn't there. I had no trouble looking like one of the students since several 7th and 8th graders were taller than I and almost as old.

If I had identified myself as the teacher, he'd still be telling folks about the dusty, sweaty, barefooted hillbilly teacher!

Viola Terwilliger
Belle, Missouri

Mail Carrier Is My Security

The District #45 schoolhouse, situated on a corner section in

SPECIAL DAYS

Polk County, Nebraska had four mailboxes at the intersection. The rural mail carrier of the Polk route was my brother, Clyde. I was a first-year teacher at this school. There wasn't such a thing as a telephone at the schoolhouse. A person would have to go a half-mile to the nearest farmhouse to get help in an emergency.

However, this teacher had it made! I got very ill one school day morning at about 10 o'clock. I knew the mailman would be at the mail box at about 10:30 a.m. because he was always punctual. I hurriedly wrote him a note about my illness to be delivered to my mother, and put it in a sealed envelope that I happened to have in my desk drawer.

Before too long, I heard the hoof of our dependable white mare outside. My mother was in the buggy as was my older sister, Blanche. Blanche was the teacher for my understanding pupils the rest of the day. I returned home with mother and I recall how wonderful that dear feather bed felt when I got to lay down.

Hazel Hill
Polk, Nebraska

Pilot Delighted Onlookers

In the depression year of 1932 I taught in a one room county school several miles from even a small town.

One lovely spring day a little boy was enjoying the view from the window by his desk. He called out "Look! A plane is going to land in the schoolyard!" I could see a small plane flying low heading right for the schoolhouse. I hurried the children out of the house. We all stood in a group to watch.

The considerate pilot no doubt could see twenty eager little children and a teacher that did not often get to watch a plane flying.

While all eyes were watching, the plane flew over us, turned around, and started doing the flying tricks that people in our area would have had to go miles to see.

After some flying stunts the plane flew back over the group, dipped one wing and flew on to the north.

That thoughtful pilot will never know the happiness he gave that little group.

> Evelyn Hamilton
> Pleasanton, Kansas

Games Of Chance

I will try to describe some of the events such as booths for chance and cake walks. Chance was a major attraction at the carnivals. Children would set up booths and people would try their luck, just as they do today. Some of the prizes given away were odd dishes, small boxes of kleenex and other small objects that people didn't need anymore. They would have lipstick, pins and beads, handkerchiefs, powder and balloons.

Cake walks were another attraction. People brought cakes and they would be given away by playing a game. The people participating would then stand on or behind the numbers. When the music began, the people began walking around the numbers. When the music stopped, all the people stopped walking and the person standing on or behind the number of the cake would win the cake.

> Georgia Callen
> Amazonia, Missouri

One Dollar – Two Dollar – Three Dollar – Sold!

One year we had a box supper after our program. Each girl was to make a box and fill it with food. My mother and I worked for days to make a pretty box. We covered it with blue crepe paper and pretty rufflers. My mother fixed fried chicken, sandwiches, two bananas (which was special because we seldom had them), chocolate cake, and, to top it all off, two Milky Way candy bars. The big night came and I was so excited, I just knew some certain boy would buy my box. A neighbor acted as auctioneer. There were several boxes to be sold - finally he picked up mine. The bidding began at a dollar, then a dollar and a quarter, and progressed to three dollars then at three and a

quarter the bidding stopped. Guess who bought my box? My Dad! There we sat on a bench, my Dad happy as a lark enjoying the good food, but I can't say the same for me. When we got home my Mother told Dad he wasn't supposed to have bought my box and he said he couldn't see why not. He wasn't going to let someone else eat all the good food, besides he paid good money for it!
Marie Holzwarth
St. Francis, Kansas

Lost Appetite For Pie

I would set the date at mid-winter 1928. There was always money raised at a pie and box supper. After the program they picked a friend of ours from St. Joe to sell the pies. He was busy with his selling and I and a friend were just looking on and listening. He called for a dollar bid and I said, a louder than I meant to, "A dollar!" I had no intention of bidding, as I had no money with me at the age of 10. As I recall that was a lot of money back then!

Well, our friend heard me say that and down went the hammer. Pointing right at me he said, "Sold to the little boy over there!"

I thought I was going to fall through the floor! But I didn't. As it turned out it was the teacher's pie, and he paid for it and ate with her. I didn't have any appetite for pie that evening!
Marion McMillion
Apple Valley, California

Birthday Spanks

Birthdays were special at school. You brought a treat. You got spinned in the teacher's chair and "spanked" for the number of years you were.
Carmel McCloskey
Racine, Wisconsin

MY FOLKS AND THE ONE-ROOM SCHOOLHOUSE

Box Social

I once fixed a box in the shape of a ladies shoe — pink and white — with a draw-string at the top and also a pink bow — a very pretty and different box! No one was to ever tell whose box it was. The man would sit with the lady whose box he bought and eat the packed lunch. Besides the fellowship, the auction also brought in money for the district school supplies.

When my box was held up for auction, a school board member, Harvey Hahn, bid on it first. Immediately my boyfriend gave him competition because he then knew it was the teacher's basket. Believe me they bid that box to the unbelievable amount of $14.25! My boyfriend was the highest bidder.

(Incidentally, he is now my husband of 60 years and we still chuckle about that box social. My daughter has the basket yet, although it was made in 1929.)

Hazel Hill
Polk, Nebraska

Time Out For Bloomers

At that time, mothers made their daughters bloomers of black sateen. (A shiny black cotton material.)

At noon hour, the boys and girls had a baseball game. This one day, a girl was running to the bases when the rubber in her black bloomers broke. They started going down around her legs. She pulled them up, ran to the girls outhouse and took them off. Then she came back to the ball game to resume playing.

When we laugh about this, I say they had to have time out for the bloomers.

Erminnie Hoenes
Marshall, Michigan

The Joys Of A Pie Supper

The one-room school was the setting for the pie supper. To me it was a strange and wonderful place, hinting of mysteries unknown. Anyway, the pie supper was a money-raising activity.

SPECIAL DAYS

The ladies took great care in baking their favorite or prize pies. Then they fairly outdid themselves in wrapping and decorating them in gaily hued crepe paper. The kind of pie (apple, cherry, butterscotch, banana cream, you name it) was written on a slip of paper and placed on the outside of the wrapping. The name of the PIE-MAKER on its slip of paper was carefully concealed INSIDE the wrapping. That was part of the fun!

The unmarried girls had the opportunity to show what good cooks they were and who's to know whether or not a favorite swain was let into the secret that "her" pie was the one with the red and yellow paper roses! And all being fair in love, if the same information was slipped to more than one Lochinvar so that the two would bid against each other, that was even more fun, as well as more money for the good cause.

The married women also had a little variety added to their lives because after the pies had been auctioned off, the purchaser peeked inside to see whose pie he had bought. The maker of the pie already knew, of course, and was ready with plates and napkins, knives and forks, and the two sat together and ate the pie. I always wanted my mother to dress up her pie in fancy paper, but she always wrapped it neatly in gray or brown wrapping paper, and Daddy always bought it. Where was their sense of romance, thought I, foolish child that I was!

My Daddy was the auctioneer and I was always so proud of him. Everybody liked him and he was much sought after for those occasions.

The joys of the pie supper were remembered even unto my high school days and I wrote a poem about it, for which I received the grade of "A."

I went to a pie supper the other night
When the rim of the golden moon hung low
And I found the answer to this maiden's prayer
In the fourth seat in the row.

The scene was in a schoolhouse

Far out from the town
Ah! his hair is dark and curly
And his eyes are soft and brown.

The auctioneer held up my pie -
"Ah, boys, you bought too soon;
This here pie's a masterpiece!"
I gazed at the golden moon.

My Romeo sprang from his seat;
"Two bit! Two bits!" he said.
Oh, I will remember that
Until I am cold and dead.

After the selling was over
He close beside me sat.
We cut the pie and ate it
And talked of this and that.

My heart was growing fonder
But I no longer tarried,
When with a sinking heart
I learned that he was married!

Marcia Baker Pogue
Cincinnati, Ohio

Reprinted with permission from *The Ohio Southland.*

Pies And Pickles

Pie suppers were always important events in the "good ol' days" of the one-room school. Proceeds were often used to provide Christmas treats for everyone in the district as well as all who had brought pies or boxes. And the rivalry was great! Even in the middle of the depression, boxes went for the outlandish sums of eight and ten dollars. The teacher had the unique position of having her box be in demand, and her box brought the highest price, at least mine did that year. Another feature was the box of chocolates for the most popular girl. This was regarded as an honor indeed, that is, if the boy friends provided

SPECIAL DAYS

the funds, and not father or brothers! Then there was a jar of pickles for the most love-sick couple, sometimes bona fide, and sometimes for two who just couldn't abide each other. And last the bar of soap for the man with the dirtiest feet, something to be received with great, good humor, or get the name of being a poor sport.

Edith Thiessen
Collinsville, Oklahoma

CHAPTER 10: From the Teacher

Love And Concern Abundant

Memories of the one-room school are pleasant and vivid in my mind. My first encounter with school was for eight years as a student in the one-room school.

Later I taught nine years in the one-room school. Life was simple and pleasant. I was visiting with a former schoolmate last evening and we agreed that we really received a good education in the old school. We cited how well we learned our math, reading and geography. Also the successes of former students in later life. Many have become wealthy in worldly possessions. Many have become inventors, shown talents in our modern society. We see doctors, nurses, ministers, aviators and many useful positions in our world. We learned to become skaters, mud waders and athletes on our way to school. We received our physical education on our way to school by sliding, trudging through snow, mud and cold. We fell, picked ourselves up and learned to go on. I remember seeing the sunrise in the Eastern sky in the morning and saw it set in the West from the schoolroom when I taught.

Once we had a terrible blizzard during the day. The snow was deep. One frail boy had to walk across the field over fences to his home. I was afraid he couldn't find his way through the blowing snow so I took him by the hand and took him home before I went to my abode. Love and concern was abundant in those days.

Ida Marie Jones
Mountain View, Missouri

The Superintendent's Surprise

County superintendents are the fear of the rural teacher and here is a story of his visit:

I was teaching in this rural school, which had a lean-to filled with coal and kindling. A neighbor's dog was always getting into it and causing all kinds of confusion. One day I was having class; there was quite a commotion in the lean-to. I turned to the children and said, "Just a moment, there's that pesky dog again and I'm going to let him have what's coming to him." I opened the door to a surprised (and so was I) county superintendent. I don't know who was more embarrassed, he or I. He came in, sat down in a chair, and whirled the ring on his finger again and again. I tried to conduct school as usual but it wasn't easy. He stayed until school was dismissed and after all the children were gone. Surprise of all surprises, he asked me for a date. I must have done something right.

Nelle Gilg
Atkinson, Nebraska

Eyes In The Back Of Her Head

In my junior year of college I was home for Easter vacation, and my grandfather brought two strange gentlemen to our house. After introductions and some small talk, including a few personal questions, they told me that they needed a schoolteacher for their one-room country school near Sheldon, Missouri, starting next September. Imagine my surprise when they offered me the job! A contract was produced and I was hired then and there for nine months at the gigantic salary of $25.00 a month.

My most memorable day at this school involved a couple of darling six-year-old twins, just starting school. I always demanded quiet in my schoolroom so the students and I could concentrate. One of the twins was quite a "talker" and she had a pronounced lisp even when she whispered. One day I was writing a lesson on the blackboard with my back to the students. Soon I heard this little lisping whisperer telling her twin sister something. Without even turning I said, "Georgie, you must be quiet. Remember the rules!" There was utter silence for a bit, then the question, "Miss Dene, how did you know it wasss me?" I replied, "Because I have eyes in the back of my head." And that took care of things.

The next morning a very irate parent was waiting for me at the door of the schoolhouse, demanding to know why I was telling my students baloney like I had eyes in the back of my head!

I probably learned a lot more during those two delightful years of teaching a country school than the children did!
Evelyn Sooy
San Diego, California

Lessons Of Life

I used Life Buoy soap at school for medication. I used cotton to cleanse scratches; but we didn't have many injuries.

Objectives of Self-Realization, Human Relationships, Economic Efficiency, and Civic Responsibility were stressed.

I learned kindness, compassion, sincereness, genuineness, courage, honesty, fairness, determination, encouragement and many more qualities during my first year of teaching.
Gertrude Rouggly
Flat River, Missouri

Directional Decimal

I'm sure that all rural teachers remember some of the cute things said by their pupils.

In the examination sent out by the state every two months, the second graders were asked to write the Flag Salute.

FROM THE TEACHER

We said the Flag salute and the Lord's Prayer every morning.
One little second grader wrote, with a few misspelled words,
"I pledge allegiance to the flag of the United States of America. And to the Republic for which it stands,
Give us this day our daily bread with liberty and justice for all. Amen."

Then there was the fifth grade boy who knew well how to multiply and divide decimals by 10, 100, etc. His problems were correct every day, and when I corrected his papers, I could see that he was moving the decimal point from the right to the left.

But when an examination asked the rule he wrote, "When you multiply a decimal by ten, move the decimal point one place to the east; when you divide a decimal by ten just move the decimal point one place to the west." It worked, as his desk faced north!

Mrs. Irvan (Harriet) Moore
Osage City, Kansas

Teacher Married Student

My uncle learned more than readin', 'ritin' and 'rithmetic in a one-room school. He learned to love his teacher (my aunt) enough to marry her!

She had planned to marry a young man that tragically died of typhoid. Uncle was almost ten years younger than my aunt but she seemed as young or younger. They raised two children and we were together a lot as we always lived within visiting distance of each other. We also saw them a lot at family gatherings.

Jewell Cooper
Bolivan, Missouri

The Case Of The Missing Cap

In 1929 I was teaching country school and this may be of interest to you. One day it turned really cold and Kenneth, a first grader, could not find his cap when it was time to go home so I had all of the children looking in the outhouses, etc., and none of us could find his cap. So I put my scarf on him and when he got home his mother came right up and really gave me a #1 scolding for not finding his cap and was going to have me fired right away. She went to the director and soon as she did, he came and told me not to let it bother me and not to worry.

Well, guess what? The next day here came Kenneth to school with his cap on and I asked where did he find his cap. He said, "In my boot!" You see he was from poor people and had to wear boots, etc. of his brothers. No, the mother never did come and apologize.

Alice Jenkins
Lamoni, Iowa

Rules For Teachers

Female teachers were not allowed to wear long pants, but I had a wool melton "Ski Suit," with knit cuffs on the bottoms of the legs that I wore over my skirts and removed before the children made an appearance. No teacher was permitted to smoke on the school grounds, and every teacher's behavior had to be above reproach.

Reva E. Seckington
Marshall, Missouri

Teacher's Wardrobe

I had dreamed for many years and planned to become a schoolteacher, as my mother and grandfather had been. I wanted to join the profession, too. I had always loved school and wanted to teach children.

We were not blessed with much money - no one else, it seems, was either. The summer after I graduated from the country high school, where my brother and I both finished, I attended the summer session at Southwestern State Teachers' College (the name of the institution is now Southwestern State University).

I had never owned many clothes - only what I needed, so it was not much of a problem for me to move to the Coffey's to begin school. Mom and I did enjoy getting my wardrobe together as we had done for my college days. I did a lot of my own

sewing and wore mostly skirts and blouses with maybe a sweater or two. I wore long cotton hose, or anklets sometimes for school, and low-heeled walking shoes (penny loafers or saddle oxfords). I bought some clothing, I did buy a blue all-weather coat to wear to school, for I walked and was in and out of all kinds of weather. We did have nylon hose to wear, only for good, but they were not like the nice ones we have now. They even had seams down the back, which were difficult to keep straight. No lady, at this time, ever wore slacks, pants or jeans. Teachers began wearing them in the '60s, and it was difficult for some of us to accept and wear them. There have been so many changes in modes of dress!
Sibyl Webb
Hinton, Oklahoma

Ode To A County Superintendent

One of the scary things I remember during both my student and teacher days was the visit from the county superintendent. This lady would drop in, unexpectedly if possible, like the proverbial thief-in-the-night to learn if the teacher was following the prescribed course of study or wandering down some avenue of learning not recognized by the authorities.

During one of my teaching years, everything seemed to go wrong the day the CS dropped in. That night I couldn't sleep and these lines flew into my head:

With Apologies To Poe
Today is dark and dreary as March days often are.
In my bones I sense some trouble in the future not too far.

What can it be, I wonder, that is lurking my way?
Will I know what 'tis I'm dreading before I've lived the day?

Thus I ponder, ponder, ponder, but I ponder it no more.
For the County Superintendent is a-standing at the door!

I know she will not hurt me, but my senses all have left.
I'm really scared quite spit-less, of my speech I am bereft.

She quietly sits, smiling, but I close my eyes and "squench"
For just where she is sitting there is coal dust on the bench.

There quite cozily beside her the wash basin sits
And tells a vivid story of some mighty dirty mits.

Someone dropped the soap jar, floor's slick as a banana.
And there for every eye to see is dust on the pianna.

My precious little darlings with their talents all so rare
Must vie at making noises so she'll know that they are there.

Why must they drop their pencils,
Squeak their shoes and slam their books,
And why above all these things must they give her coy looks?

As I view their strange behavior, I vow they will repent,
But shall I knock their teeth out now, or wait till she "has went?"
                        Marjorie Crouch
                        Uvalde, Texas

Happy Memories Outweigh Bad

I graduated from high school in 1939, at the age of 17, and began teaching a rural school that fall. We started out with a 3rd grade Elementary certificate and had to renew it every 3 years, usually by attending summer school sessions at a nearby college.

My pupils numbered anywhere from three second graders one year to 16 pupils in kindergarten through eighth grade.

My most unusual experience was the year two pupils, a 3rd grade girl and an 8th grade boy from Nuremburg, Germany, attended my school along with 14 others from the district. They were among the displaced people arriving from Europe after World War II. Their parents worked for a local farmer to reimburse him for sponsoring their trip to Nebraska. These two pupils couldn't speak English and I didn't know a word of German. Fortunately they were very intelligent and soon adapted to our ways. In order to teach them English, I used the Dick and Jane primers, teaching them one word at a time and pointing to objects in the room, giving it the English name. I was very proud that the 8th grade boy was able by the next spring to pass his 8th grade exams, and enroll in the local high school.

One of my memories during the Nebraska blizzard of 1947, there was so much snow, it was almost an impossibility to get to school. I drove an unheated Model A Ford. When I got to school, the snow was banked up so high in front of the door, I couldn't get in. After several minutes of shoveling, I finally got in the door. Snow banks were as high as the schoolhouse, so the pupils had much fun at recesses, sledding and climbing up and down the hills.

One of my schools didn't have a well, so it was up to the teacher to provide the water. I boarded with my grandmother, and carried a 3-gallon aluminum pail of water to school every morning. Instead of going around the road, I took a shortcut by crossing through fields and crawling under several fences with my pail. In very frigid weather there were times the water began freezing in the pail. At the end of the year I was rewarded for my services with an extra $5 in my paycheck. I also furnished an alarm clock, since the school didn't have one.

As I look back over the years, the happy memories outweigh the few bad ones, and many of my pupils still keep in touch.

Virginia Oates
Exeter, Nebraska

Dog Provides Escort

Every rural schoolteacher who was hired in a new district found that she was expected to give a complete background during the opening hour of the first day of school.

Pupils wanted to know her age, name, religion, number of children if she was married, and if she was going to be "crabby."

It only took a day or two in a new position to determine the kind of home each child came from. Sometimes the circumstances were heart-breaking as somehow the teacher became a confidante as little hearts overflowed.

Perhaps one event stands out in my memory more than others. The sheriff had stopped to ask me to keep the door locked all day because a criminal had been spotted on the highway. Naturally I was a bit fearful each morning as I drove into the yard, not knowing what I might find.

Across the road lived the family of one pupil and their dog was notorious for taking a nip at anyone who got out of their car. However, sensing danger, that dog met me at my car and escorted me to the door every day. One morning I found beer cans, food wrappers and orange peels on the steps - so we had had visitors.

Thus is the lore of an ex-teacher who loved every minute spent in a rural school.

Madonna Kellar Storla
Postville, Iowa

Cleaning Tissues

In my early grade school days, and even sometimes when teaching in the '20s, youngsters came to school with NEVER a handkerchief or even a rag.

The girls wiped their noses on their skirt-tails and the boy wiped theirs on their shirt sleeves!

As young ladies, a fine linen handkerchief was the final touch to our attire as we prepared to "step out" with our "beaus"...or to go to church.

Handkerchiefs were always white. We could buy regular handkerchief linen by the yard. A yard would make nine. They could be hand hemstitched or roll stitched, all embroidered and with either crocheted or tatted lace edging. So elegant!

Ready made handkerchiefs could be purchased for five or ten cents — up to 25¢ for a real nice linen one.

For every day use men and boys carried huge red or blue figured handkerchiefs — used nowadays for headgear, neck scarves, decorations of all kinds — everything except to blow your nose on.

FROM THE TEACHER

During the Depression we even made everyday men's handkerchiefs out of salt sacks, the tails of old white shirts (when we didn't have so much as a dime or a nickel to buy them) and a soft old undershirt tail was just the thing to take to bed with you if you had a bad cold!

Now days Kleenex solves all our "nose" problems.

Muriel Razor
Wadesville, Indiana

(Editor's Note: Mrs. Razor passed away in January, 1993. Her letter was submitted in her memory by Myron D. Razor.)

Share And Share Alike

During part of the years I was teaching, I had three sisters teaching at the same time. We all stayed at home with our one car and we'd drop one off at a time to four different schools. We planned our lessons and programs together (this was during the Depression, too). At Christmas time we would buy one Christmas tree, each planning our Christmas program on different nights so we could move the Christmas tree to each school. Then we'd take it home and decorate it for our family on Christmas Eve for our folks.

Emilie Bird
Beatrice, Nebraska

Fire In The Hole

My husband was not sent to school until shortly after his seventh birthday.

The teacher told him where to sit but did not give him anything to do. He listened for quite awhile to the older students doing their lessons, but he got bored with nothing to do so he just got up and walked home. Nobody had explained to him that you have to wait to be dismissed by the teacher.

Many years later he taught in a school. He smoked cigarettes at that time and one noon he went into the basement for a quick smoke. He didn't want his students to see him smoke - bad

MY FOLKS AND THE ONE-ROOM SCHOOLHOUSE

example; but he heard two of his fourth grade boys coming down the stairs and put the cigarette in his pants pocket. Shortly, one of the boys became excited, saying, "Teacher, your pants are on fire!"

Jane Waldroop
Norman, Oklahoma

Quiet As A Mouse

My Aunt was a teacher in a one room rock schoolhouse built in 1885 and is still standing in 1992. She was in an automobile wreck and they asked my Mother to teach for her.

We didn't know about babysitters in those days, so Mother took me, a three-year-old, to school.

She said I sat very quietly and hardly knew I was there.

She always took me to Normal (teacher training in the '30s) with her. She said I always sat very quietly and gave her no bother!

Pauline Fecht
Syracuse, Kansas

Repetition Works Well

I had six grades, not including fourth or sixth if I remember right, and only thirteen or fourteen pupils. There was a "recitation bench" near the teacher's desk so that she could call each class up to recite. There were only 5 to 7 minutes for each class depending on the number of grades. Some classes such as civics and physiology had to be divided into twice a week and three times a week.

On Fridays, after the last recess, we would have a spelling bee or map hunt or ciphering match. On the map hunts, a young child would sit down with an older one and someone would write the name of a town, river or mountains on the board and the rest of the school would try to be the first to find it on the map in the geography book.

If there were any exceptionally bright older children who had time, you could let them take a younger one aside to help him

FROM THE TEACHER

with his reading, etc. Fourth and fifth-graders could drill first and second graders on flash cards. Crossword puzzles were good for older pupils after finishing lessons.

Often a bright child's education was enhanced by attending a one-room school. The young ones, as they came up in grades, could get facts and ideas firmly entrenched in their minds by listening to the older classes recite and by watching them work math on the blackboard so that it came very easy to them when they reached the higher grades. The old principle of repetition worked very well here.

One class that I held two or three times a month was on diacritical markings. Many grown people say they never learned in school how to pronounce words from the markings used in the dictionary.

In March I let the eighth graders know that I would expect a summary of each of their subjects to be written up on several pages of notebook paper along with illustrations and finished with an attractive cover for display on a table to be turned in two weeks before the end of school.

Their "graduation" depended on their good summaries and grades, of course.

Crystal Bennett Edwards
Anderson, Missouri

Cautious Class

Teaching in a one-room school was never without surprises.

On a busy highway, the schoolhouse faced south so we were not aware of the events to the east of us.

One of the boys went out to display the flag and very quietly called me to the cloakroom.

"There's a man sitting on the approach to the schoolyard. He has a package on his lap which looks like a rifle that is not assembled."

Needless to say, the door was locked immediately and no one left the building until the parents came to pick up their children. We did not mention the problem so the younger ones would not panic and cause a lot of pandemonium in the room.

After school was dismissed, one of the parents and an older lad looked into the culvert and found empty wrappers for food, pop and pieces of bread. Apparently someone was using it for a place to sleep.

The next morning after the bell had rung, I peered out the bathroom window. Lo and behold, he was back!

During the forenoon, I glanced down the road and a man was going under a bridge where a small stream of water flowed. In a few minutes I saw the reflection of a mirror. In all probability, he was shaving.

We notified the sheriff, but the highway patrol had spotted him first. Actually he was not guilty of any crime, but he was homeless and broke. The patrolman asked him to unwrap the package. It contained a fishing rod which had been dismantled!

Madonna K. Storla
Postville, Iowa

(Editor's Note: Mrs. Storla also reports that soon after the director had a phone installed for the teacher!)

Unexpected Visitor

At the close of a busy day teaching twenty-six pupils in my one-room school, I did my janitorial duties. The wooden floor was sprinkled with a red cleaning compound, then swept with a wide-width broom; the three gallon crock jug was filled with fresh water from the pump outside which I sometimes had to prime; the across-the-room blackboard was cleaned by going vertically across the board with an eraser, then wiping that eraser with a cloth after each stroke. I went to the stove and put over my right arm a sleeve made from my Dad's worn-out overall leg so when I opened the stove door and raked down the fire I wouldn't get soot on my blouse. I put the empty coal bucket by the door. I dusted the window sills and made sure all the windows were locked by turning a latch fastened in the middle of the window pane, and then dusted the recitation bench. Last, I made the journey to the two outhouses to make sure there was a supply of paper — catalogue or newspapers — for the next day, and closed the doors securely.

I then went to the coalhouse with the empty bucket and filled it, taking it back into the school building. Ah! After my school duties were done, and school papers were in my home bag to be corrected, I stepped back and admired my Thanksgiving-decorated schoolroom. How I loved the energetic children and this schoolhouse! I locked the schoolhouse door.

Early Wednesday morning, my mother took me in a one-horse drawn buggy three miles to my school. It was a very cold November day and snow was on the ground. The chilly wind told me I'd need to build a very warm fire before the children arrived to warm the schoolroom.

After telling my mother thanks (she taught at this same school before she married,) and unlocking the door, I stepped into the room. Was I ever surprised! The room was warm. There was a good fire going in the stove. I wondered what had happened. Glancing around the room my eyes spotted a nicely written note on the blackboard. It read:

"Thanks for a good night's rest and for a warm
room. I refilled the coal bucket. Forgive me for eating the apple
and candy you had in your desk.
Tell the kids to work hard and learn—knowledge is power."
A Thankful Tramp

I often wondered about the unseen visitor. How did he get into the room? Why he turned out as a tramp when his writing indicated he was educated, and the room was left in perfect condition, I guess I will never know.

Hazel Hill
Polk, Nebraska

Teaching Learned Early

My school years 1928-29 and 29-30 were as a junior and a senior in high school, and were almost entirely devoted to prepare me to teach a one-room school.

We memorized many poems that all students for years had

learned. When we did this, all in that class would study it for a few minutes, then the whole school would repeat it aloud until they had it pretty well.

All but the first and second graders memorized all twelve multiplication tables.

After a teacher taught in a rural school for three years, we were eligible to teach in the town school at a higher wage for usually one grade (versus all grades).

Jerry Tudgay
Osage City, Kansas

Teaching Appreciated By All

I was sixteen years old, just graduated from High School, passed the teacher's Normal Training Examinations given at the county courthouse, and received my teaching certificate. How happy I was to be hired to teach the fall term in the school where my mother and two sisters had taught.

That first school day in September, when I was the TEACHER, will never be forgotten. I had all eight grades, some students much larger physically than I. It was a challenge.

At four o'clock, after the children left to walk home, I found three scribbled notes on my desk...each one said "I like you."

Another thrill happened in the spring. My wages the past year had been 80 dollars a month. A mother wanted me to be sure to teach the following year and she told me if the School Board didn't raise my wages sufficiently the mothers of the district would band together and increase my salary considerably. It wasn't necessary. I stayed, and although the one-room country schoolhouse has been removed, I worked forty years (off and on) bit by bit to get a B.S. Degree, and after 50 years I'm still teaching because I love it.

Hazel Hill
Polk, Nebraska

(Editor's Note: This letter was written to *Capper's* in 1979. But, Hazel Hill is still substitute teaching at age 80!)

INDEX

A

Aalbers, Mrs. Tone 36
Allen, Helen 16
Anton, Lucille 33
Arentson, Hester 83
Armstrong, Mrs. Robert 55
Armstrong, Roscoe E. vi
Atkinson, Betty Jane 103

B

Bailey, Nova Felkins 51
Bainbridge, Theresa 77
Bashford, Wanda Wolf 76
Beatty, Donna 17
Bergstrom, Mrs. Gus 25
Bird, Emilie 66, 127
Blevins, Blanche (Silvey) 8, 63
Boeckmann, Lucinda 45
Boertje, Helen Van Zante 106
Bowers, Leola 95
Boyd, Mrs. Paul 31
Brant, Euna Vaye Ukena 58
Brennan, Bertha Elizabeth 74
Brown, V.F. 81

C

Callen, Georgia 112
Cantrell, Edna Flanary 19
Cardin, Matilda Winters 100
Carmann, Dorothy 13, 24, 28, 50, 68
Carr, Elaine 29, 55
Carroll, Emma May Schell 58
Carson, Eugene 35
Clements, Thelma 109
Clifford, Della May 5, 21
Cook, Gladys 10

Cooper, Jewell 36, 121
Crouch, Marjorie 24, 57, 124
Croy, Helen 17
Culp, Dortha 12

D

Darnell, Carol 47, 87, 100
Deason, Mildred 108
Densford, Edna 45
Derendinger, Elaine 47
Dernell, Betty 12

E

Eason, Nina 42
Easter, Edna 39, 102
Edwards, Crystal Bennett 129
Eli, Vera J. 20

F

Fecht, Pauline 94, 128
Feyerherm, Olga (Huntemann) 89
Fluit, Brenda 39
Fuller, Evelina 9

G

Gallatin, Verna 13
Gardener, Mary 63
Gaylord, Mary 78
Gettys, Sarah Mitchell 15
Gilbert, Lola 12, 75
Gilg, Nelle 119
Gohr, Hazel 22
Goodman, Marjorie 90
Grube, Eileen 92
Gump, Frances 70

INDEX

H

Hamilton, Evelyn 112
Hardy, Elizabeth 101
Harrison, J. Carl 94
Hensley, Tiny 96
Heyn, Mercedes 82
Hill, Hazel 111, 114, 131, 132
Hoenes, Erminnie 114
Holzwarth, Marie 113
Hughes, Ola M. 86

I

Ingels, Claracy 109

J

Jacobs, Helen 109
Jenkins, Alice 89, 122
Jincks, Ruth 97
Jobst, Mrs. Raymond 16
Jones, Ida Marie 119
Jump, Lena 6

K

Kenkel, Fern 67
Kirby, Emmett 42
Kisby, Astrid 108
Klahn, Dorothy 65
Kristiansen, Jean 80
Krone, Floranna 53
Kump, Carl 76
Kunkle, William 56

L

Lanz, Bessie 31
Larson, Jeannette 70
Leppert, Clara 52
Lewis, Esther 42

M

Markovetz, Hazel Hoyt 92
Martin, Maithel Davenport ...37
Mason, Alice R. 83
Massey, Gerald D. 71
Maxwell, Edward 81
Mayes, Earline 34
McCloskey, Carmel 113
McGowin, Marjorie Burd 78
McMillion, Marion 113
Messick, Mrs. Moody 67
Meyer, Henry J. 62
Millenbruch, Hazel 74, 91
Moore, Harriet (Mrs. Irvan) .121

N

Nicholson, Davida 7, 64

O

Oates, Virginia 125
Oliver, Mrs. Glen 61

P

Palmer, Florence 7, 50
Penner, Marladeen ...25, 32, 40
Pogue, Marcia Baker 116
Priddy, Lorraine 93

INDEX

Q

Queen, Barbara 23, 90

R

Razor, Muriel 127
Riley, Jeneal 69
Robertson, O.J. 26
Robinson, Hope 49
Rouggly, Gertrude 76, 120

S

Schneider, Marguerite 56
Schwynock, Kathrine ...73, 102
Seager, Ralph W. 60
Seckington, Reva 122
Sexton, Helen 85
Shockley, Pearl 88
Snaza, Eileen 21
Sooy, Evelyn 120
Storla, Madonna 43, 79, 80, 126, 130
Swinford, Mildred 62
Sybrant, Gladys 43

T

Terwilliger, Viola 110
Thiessen, Edith 117
Toliver, Gladys 53
Trail, Frances Hoyt 22
Tudgay, Jerry 132
Turner, Glenna 98

U

Utecht, Delores 105

V

Vance, Helen 68

W

Waldren, Mildred Jones ...52, 96
Waldroop, Jane 128
Walker, Mrs. Guyneth 61
Warren, Inez 30
Webb, Sibyl 104, 123
Welborn, Jean Carpenter 44
Wells, Vera 34
Whitesell, Della 4
Whobrey, Annabel 17
Willcut, Edith 66
Williamson, Thelma 41
Wilson, Berniece 69
Winn, Cecil Utterback 28
Wonnell, Rex 3
Woodward, William 110
Worley, Mary 98
Wyatt, Imogene 31

Y

Young, Velma C. 71

136